# ROCK AND ROLL

Other books by Paul Williams:

Outlaw Blues
Bob Dylan, Performing Artist (Vols I & II)
The Map, or Rediscovering Rock and Roll
Das Energi
Only Apparently Real: The World of Philip K. Dick
Remember Your Essence
Apple Bay
Heart of Gold
Waking Up Together
The International Bill of Human Rights (editor)
Common Sense
Nation of Lawyers
The Book of Houses (with Robert Cole)
Pushing Upward
Dylan—What Happened?
Coming
Time Between
Right to Pass

# ROCK AND ROLL
# THE 100 BEST SINGLES

Paul Williams

Carroll & Graf Publishers, Inc.
New York

First Carroll & Graf edition 1993

Carroll & Graf Publishers, Inc.
260 Fifth Avenue
New York, NY 10001



Library of Congress Cataloging-in-Publication Data

Williams, Paul, 1948–
Rock and roll : the 100 best singles / Paul Williams.
—1st Carroll & Graf ed.
p. cm.
ISBN 0-88184-966-9 (paper) : $10.95
1. Rock music—History and criticism. I. Title.
MI3534.W6 1933
781.66—dc20 92-47502
CIP
MN

Manufactured in the United States of America

for Richard Glyn Jones,
in spite of everything,
and for my dancer and my singer

# Contents

# INTRODUCTION

## by Cindy Lee Berryhill

Paul W. asked me to write an introduction to his *100 Best Singles of Rock and Roll.* (I thought he was joking.) I'd never written one before, but when I got to thinking about it I figured this out . . . it should start with a BANG! This is what invites the reader to the show. In a respect it's being the opening act. I'm a musician, I've done that before. I've opened up for a number of different musical acts like X, Roger McGuinn, and the Butthole Surfers, but this is my first time opening for an author.

Rather: author, journalist, fan, wacked-out philosopher, publisher of sorts . . . all those things, some others, too. I met Paul W. at a Bob Dylan concert this past spring. A music friend introduced us. I knew his writing from some old *Crawdaddy!* articles reproduced in a Xerox book (called *The Dumb Angel Gazette*) about Brian Wilson's forlorned *Smile.* But this couldn't be that guy, the guy that wrote that old '60's stuff and started that prehistoric r&r mag (*Crawdaddy*). This guy didn't have any of that burnt-out look you get accustomed to seeing in a lotta rock people from its big revolutionary era. You know, like: "Kid don't bother me with anything new now I've seen it all!" (You hear the sound of a door slamming.) Or, the "freedom rock" thing: "I just love all kinds of music, everything, anything, and I love you." (They've been too new age-ified to have any opinion or taste.)

I went back to my date and friends and told them about my good fortune in meeting this rock and roll, Navy-issue/physicist-glasses guy. There was some explaining to do cuz when I told them "Paul Williams" they all chimed in, "Oh, the dwarf." I think *that* Paul Williams is much more known for his appearances on the Carson show than his songwriting. Meanwhile: after the Dylan show a bunch of people were hanging out in the lobby of the Pantages Theater comparing napkins. Paul W. was there, so was my friend and some other guys, they were all jabbering about what songs Dylan had sung, and believe me it took a good ear to figure out what was what (Bob D. had changed all the old melodies, so the songs sounded brand new/ it was a good laugh).

Paul W. and I spoke further and decided to meet the following day for lunch at Canter's. It was just one of those real cool r&r things, meeting him.

The next day I kept thinking as me and my VW bus chugged toward Fairfax: What am I doing going to meet some guy I don't even know? What are we going to talk about, maybe he'll think I'm some geeky r&r fan and all that stupid stuff that goes on in yer head when you do something new.

Paul W. was there already, in a booth I'd seen Peter Case sitting in a year before. He had a ratty notebook I mistook for a journal ("No, it's not a journal") and a big pile of loose papers with typewriting all over. We said hello, ordered sandwiches, then he gave me a list of a bunch of rock and roll songs, said to pick one. I picked. "Heroes and Villains."

Paul W. pushed his nerd glasses further up his nose. He had a funny look on his face, a sort of perpetual smile, I couldn't tell if it was just the shape of his mouth or if he was always sort of laughing at life. But when he read out loud he got real serious with the Spock eyebrow-raise and long dramatic pauses between sentences.

I mean, it was a crack-up. Oh, don't get me wrong—not like he was a joke or anything, or even that I wanted to laugh. But the combination of his oratory dramatics, the emphatic hands, the Isaac Asimov glasses, and the stuff he was reading about was, like . . . what's going on?

Paul W. convinces you that you weren't so weird after all to think that rock and roll was a holy matter. That the right song at the right time could actually bring salvation. Well, supposedly we knew this already. For instance: "Great Balls of Fire." Jerry Lee Lewis wasn't even so sure he wanted to record this song once Sam (what's his face from Sun Records) read him the words. Jerry Lee knew God would be pissed off. He knew there was some kinda absolute power at work behind this song (I suppose Jerry thought it was the Devil in this case). And then of course there's the whole Elvis as extraterrestrial/Jesus icon. And the Dionysian "eat the seedcake" of current raves. Etc.

Well, I didn't know anyone else thought this kinda thing about popular music. Sure, a few cracked musician friends of mine. But us musicians tend to think we're healing the world anyway. Bunch o' wacked-out messiahs.

So this Paul W., how come he still loved rock and roll and why did he still look kinda like a punky high school kid and why wasn't he on musical auditory burn-out? Answer: get a grip, I don't know. Maybe rock and roll is redemptive. (I know I know tell that to Hendrix, Darby Crash, or Hillel.) I must admit, I've probably only read about half of this book. (Make that two-thirds!) This is a strange read with a title not as cool as its content. And there's a bunch of songs I wish were in here that aren't, like: the Buzzcocks, "Everybody's Happy Nowadays." The Police, "Message in a Bottle." The Replacements, "Alex Chilton." Plimsouls, "A Million Miles Away" . . . bla bla bla. We all have our lists.

The thing is, I find myself going back to certain essays on my favorite songs like "Heroes and Villains" and reading and re-reading them. I can't really explain why I'm doing this. This book has become a sort of reference for me. I find myself thinking of certain passages while working out my own songs. I feel somehow enchanted by these writings. I feel hope. I'm glad I'm a musician. Paul Williams is like the fantasy listener for us voices on CD, tape, and vinyl. Wow! this writer says what music feels like in its creation: lost and gone, a blast-off, Dante's rings of angels, too mysterious for someone like me to attempt to put into words. (Leave that to Paul W.)

I really like this book a lot (even though I still don't like "Ring My Bell." Then again, I never heard "Dark Star" before and now I love it). I hope one of my songs makes it into the next one.

My roommate thinks that I didn't end this introduction so well. Says the end should go out with a bang. He's the one that suggested the beginning start with a bang. Well, there's not too much bang going on here. But this is the end of the opening act to Paul Williams's book. I hope he sells a million copies. (Hey, do I get royalties? I mean, in music if you . . . there is the sound of a turning page.)

Cindy Lee Berryhill
Ocean Beach, October 1992

# AUTHOR'S NOTE

Everybody asks me, "What's number one?" And I explain: it's not like that, the list is chronological, starting back before the beginning and going through the '50's and the '60's and the '70's and the '80's, and ending for the sake of convenience in 1991. So #1 is not supposed to be "better" than #100. It just got in line first.

The next question has to do with criteria. My criteria are simple: the song has to have been released as a seven-inch 45 rpm single in the United States or Great Britain (Robert Johnson's 78 rpm ten-inch is the exception that proves the rule), it has to be "rock and roll" according to my subjective evaluation (I love "Oh Happy Day" by the Edwin Hawkins Singers but decided it's a pure gospel record; the fact that it was a smash hit does not of itself qualify it as great rock and roll), and I have to believe it to be good enough, stupendous enough, to be included here.

In other words, personal preference. I made this list. I believe the only true representation of what great rock and roll is lies in the experience and enthusiasm of the individual listener. Lists made by committees don't cut it. We love what we love because of our prejudices, not in spite of them, and if we try to be "objective" we take the fun out of everything, and lose sight of the truth as well.

I was seventeen years old in the summer of 1965. If I'd been born ten years earlier, this book would show a much higher proportion of selections from the '50's, and it would be just as "true" a list. If I was born ten years later . . . well, you get the idea. Truth is subjective. Music is subjective. It's supposed to be. If you want to have some fun (and some anguish), try making a "100 best singles" list of your own. You could use this one as a jumping-off place, circling keepers, crossing out rejects, question marks by the "maybe"s. If we end up with forty or fifty selections in common, we'll be doing real well.

Someone suggested I write this book, and I couldn't resist. I like to write short essays about records I love, and here was a chance to write 100 of them. Wow. Sounded like fun, and it has been. The best part has been the opportunity and obligation (some of our very favorite things in life we never do unless forced to) to listen to each of these records over and over and over, total immersion, in many cases rediscovering an intensity equal to or greater than what I felt when the song first entered my life. Again, I encourage you to try it. Pick a record and try to find out why you like it so much by listening again and again and again in rapid succession. The risk is, you may throw it against the wall and never want to hear it again (there are lots of records that started out on my list but got tossed along the way). But on the other hand you also give yourself the opportunity to experience an ecstatic breakthrough.

There's a scream inside every one of us at every moment. And every one of us has had the experience of listening to a record and feeling that scream take over. Release. Abandon. Let it all out. Rock and roll for me is about Eros, not Logos, which is paradoxical since my job is putting the experience in words. Oh, well. Hope you like it. Here we go . . .

# 1 Robert Johnson

## *Terraplane Blues*

History has nothing to do with it. Let's wipe away the romance, too, all the stuff about Johnson being seventeen years old and less than two years from death by poison at the hands of a jealous woman. Somebody should make a movie, and they did, so let's forget it, okay? Everything that matters is in the grooves. Pick it up, play it again (just as if you actually owned the 1937 Vocalion disc, with "Kind Hearted Woman" on the flip, and a 78 rpm phonograph to spin it on). Turn up the volume. It's all there.

"Mr. Highway Man, pleee-ease don't block the road." What do we hear? The guitar. The voice. The rhythm. The lyrics. What do we feel? Passion. Honesty. Pride. Fear. It's all in the grooves. And it goes straight (correct me if I'm wrong) through the needle, through the ears, into the blood, and into the heart of the listener.

I'm not saying that rock and roll begins with this incredible, prescient recording that Robert Johnson made in a hotel room in San Antonio, Texas, in November 1936. Rock and roll to me is not the sort of thing that begins and ends, or if it does, it begins in a personal way for the individual listener, like Lou Reed's Jenny:

> Then one fine morning she puts on a New York station,
> You know she don't believe what she heard at all—

and ends probably sometime long after death or else on the day you finally sell your soul irretrievably to the faceless corporate mobsters whose purpose it is to own all the vision and rhythm in the world or eradicate it, whichever comes first.

So the best rock and roll records don't really exist laid out end to end in chronological order with a preset history marching through them to bring us up to this extraordinary or (usually) all-too-ordinary moment. They exist rather in random order on a jukebox in some low dive (college snack bar, favorite pub) or as a pile of 45's on the floor, scratched and disordered, or else stacked neatly in envelopes by a compulsive collector who knows the only right way to wash and dry 'em. They exist in the mind, waiting to leap out and blind your emotions and leaden your foot on the accelerator as you turn up the radio in surprise and delight (no fun however if they play them too often and take away the cachet, the mystery). There is no key to them and you cannot make them yield their secrets, except by listening and letting yourself be carried away by whatever it was that carried away these recording artists before you.

"Terraplane Blues" is relentless. From the guitar notes that begin it, to the first words ("I feel so lonesome") to the inevitable and necessary pop hook (the little guitar twist in the payoff line—it follows the word "terraplane" the first time you hear it) to the glorious moaning bridge in the middle, to the muffled last words (like on a Rolling Stones single, you can't quite make them out; I think he's saying "your sparks're gonna give me fire"), this record drives—once or twice you can actually hear his pounding foot but mostly you just feel it, as the sole accompanying instrument slips back and forth so effortlessly between rhythm and melody, structure and elaboration, form and content, hard muscles and a pretty face. Rock and roll is sometimes a saxophone or even a synthesizer, but most of the time it's a loud guitar, with an implacable rhythm in it or behind it or both . . . and a human voice speaking not story so much as half-formed truths, phrases that cut through the limitations of ordinary language and, with the music, allow identification, allow reason to unite with emotion beyond explanation, producing truth. And when the words fail, the guitar is there, the rhythm takes over, and spirit fills in the blanks.

Robert Johnson believed in the Devil, and well he might have, sensing his own fate. In that hotel room something technological combined with something spiritual to make his existence eternal as Shakespeare's, and what I want ta know is, how do you like your brown-eyed boy, Mr. Death? Leaving history and romance out of this, of course.

*First release:* Vocalion 03416, probably early 1937

# 2 Muddy Waters

## *Rolling Stone*

Aha, you say, I've got the wrong book, this is the hundred best *blues* recordings. No no, just stay with me for a minute. There are all sorts of forerunners of rock and roll, some country, some jazz, some pop, some gospel, some blues or r&b, and I'm doing my best to ignore all of them here, due to my antihistory stance with which you are already familiar. This record, Muddy's first moderately successful single (on the r&b charts), earned its place in history by inspiring the name of one of the great rock bands, The Rolling Stones, and it also played a part in the naming of America's leading rock magazine. (It probably didn't have much to do with the title of Bob Dylan's masterpiece "Like A Rolling Stone," however—that seems to derive from the line "I'm a rolling stone, I'm alone and lost" in Hank Williams's magnificent country single "Lost Highway.") But "Rolling Stone" is in this book for one reason only: it is one of the best rock and roll singles I've ever heard, which is all the more remarkable in that it is not only pure urban blues, it is also a solo performance, just Muddy and his amplified guitar. Stick it on any modern radio station and it would sound a) out of place and b) like the hottest rocker they've played in months.

It has dignity and it kicks ass. It rocks, unquestionably; and oh God it is also the textbook example of what it means for a performance to *roll.*

The song is a self-proclaimer, part of the "look out world—members of the opposite sex especially—'cause here I come" school, which is an essential subtheme in rock and roll (even when it isn't directly in the lyrics, you can often hear it in the singer's tone of voice). Musically "Rolling Stone" draws unabashedly from Robert Johnson and Charlie Patton and their ilk, but there is also a startling leap here that effectively defines the rock and roll band sound (electric bass, drums, electric lead guitar, vocalist) even though there is no band on the record. It is as if rock and roll were an idea in Muddy Waters's head which is outlined here, a black blueprint passionately seized on by several successive white generations to come. Which Muddy predicts:

I've got a boychild coming, gonna be a rolling stone.

And while the lyrics and guitar-playing are excellent and the vocal performance superlative, what really distinguishes this recording and makes it such an irresistible listen is the *sound* (presumably producer Leonard Chess, and the gods of serendipity, also deserve a nod here).

This is the sound that, in one package or another, has captured and converted every set of young teenagers that's come along in the last thirty-five years. If there are hormones and chemicals that induce doubt, depression, and confusion in the average adolescent, there is also a particular clear echoing ring of guitar and voice, a particular pitch and form of audio intensity, that seems to be the natural counterforce and restorative. A certain sound that reaches into the electrochemical circuits of the human body and provides the energy necessary to push through this crisis of physical and emotional growth—certain chords that cut the cords and give the young human entity strength to stand on its own, confused but proud, scared but also filled with a mysterious confidence.

"Rolling Stone" precedes the general emergence of rock and roll by five years and probably didn't have much direct influence on the form until the blues-aware British burst on the scene in the 1960's. Like most of the recordings discussed in this volume, it exists outside of time. Its power relies not on aesthetic context but on its ability to speak directly to the inner emotions of the listener. And the sound that moves us most, I suspect, is not actually the guitar or the voice but the sound of the empty walls these calls in the night bounce off of. Robert Johnson and Muddy Waters are the discoverers of this sound; their pioneering efforts have been imitated and duplicated and embellished upon, but no one as far as I know has yet gone further. Perhaps that's because there is nowhere further to go.

*First release:* Chess, 1950

# 3 Little Richard

## *Tutti-Frutti*

Consider the scream. In the church—specifically the black Southern Baptist church—it not only signifies but is the experience of surrender to and unity with the Holy Spirit, an ecstatic moment in which the shackles of everyday life are shattered and an individual human voice (heart, soul) achieves and celebrates freedom. This same scream—great God Almighty, brothers and sisters, the *same* scream—comes forth from lovers' mouths during the ecstasy of sexual union. Sacred moments. The outburst in church, permitted and encouraged and indeed shared by the fellowship, the community, has the effect of making the private public, and also of conferring on the public gathering the power, intimacy, and sanctity of private revelation.

Rock and roll represents a further leap in the socialization of private experience and the simultaneous privatization and revitalization of social experience accomplished by the double-edged sword of the public scream. Little Richard's "Tutti-Frutti," his first hit single, helped tear the roof off the self-satisfied edifice called American popular music, to let in the light of unrestrained sexuality, spirituality, and musicality. Little Richard added the essential element of holy abandon. He taught us—specifically the white kids, the ones who needed to learn—how to scream.

The rest of the story is that "Tutti-Frutti" doesn't just scream; it also rocks. And this aspect of the song—communicated primarily by the band, by musical instruments rather than the human voice—is both stimulating (a real hip-shaker, irresistible) and somehow tremendously reassuring. Where "Rolling Stone" is glorious but ominous, "Tutti-Frutti" is raucous and upbeat; it beckons the listener in, to delight in the singer's hollers rather than be disturbed by them, to relax in the knowledge that this wild ecstasy is safe and friendly, a communion of good times that anyone young and free enough to own a transistor radio (it moves around with you, doesn't sit in the living room) is naturally a part of. Awrootie!

Richard Penniman was nineteen years old and already three years into a so far unsuccessful r&b recording career when he cut "Tutti-Frutti" at his first recording session for Specialty Records. The session was in New Orleans, Bumps Blackwell was the producer, and "Tutti-Frutti" was an afterthought, an obscene ditty the irrepressible Richard entertained the other musicians with between takes. The track was so hot a local songwriter had to be brought in to clean up the lyrics (originally "tutti-frutti, good booty") and make them suitable for the airwaves.

As often happens, the song that was to introduce Little Richard to the world was recorded by accident. The voice and style were his and his alone, the record captures his essential spirit, but the circumstance by which this true self got onto vinyl was unplanned, a bolt from the blue. "Wop bop alu mop a lop bomp bomp!" Speaking in tongues. Somehow this bit of lascivious horseplay, intended to amuse the other men in the room, grabbed the attention of the universe instead.

Bob Dylan was fourteen when "Tutti-Frutti" jumped out of his radio; Paul McCartney was thirteen. And nothing was the same after that. What they learned was not just a way of singing but a new angle of approach, a new possible relationship between me inside here and all of you out there. Rock and roll, born of the direct experience of the divine, became a kind of gospel of direct connection between the awesome force pent up inside the individual creator and the receptive, anonymous hunger of the new technological mass audience.

Little Richard, filled with doubt precisely equal to his amazing assertiveness, suddenly quit rock and roll after eighteen months of stardom and went off to become a preacher. Later, 1964, he returned to claim his crown as King of Rock and Roll, but of course he'd never been gone. Vinyl means immortality. The screams of Little Richard leap joyously off the turntable to this day.

*First release:* Specialty 561, November 1955

# 4 Elvis Presley

## *Heartbreak Hotel*

How can I miss you, a great philosopher* once inquired, if you won't go away? Elvis Presley is everywhere in American mass media and (what passes for) American consciousness as I write this, so much so that even jokes about his omnipresence have become tiresome. This deification of Elvis has about as much to do with rock and roll as the posthumous deification of Marilyn Monroe had to do with sex (as in actual lovemaking). In a culture where communication is achieved through marketing, symbolic image is everything. Some of us would rather worship the image of a rock and roll king than actually listen to the stuff. And of course Elvis was really a rock and roller for only a few short years, a stop on his journey from country music hopeful to packageable pop property and superstar crooner. Most of his hits were ballads.

Be that as it may, it was as a rock and roller that he made his mark, and it was through Elvis that rock and roll arrived in white America. He was the Prometheus who crossed the finish line, even if he just picked up his fire down the street in Big Mama Thornton or even Carl Perkins's neighborhoods (and—let's be fair—Elvis did add considerable fire of his own to all his best recordings). And his breakthrough record, a performance that still resonates today with all the spine-tingling power and dignity and mystery of a classic rock and roll single (weird dead-Elvis cargo cult notwithstanding), was "Heartbreak Hotel."

This was Elvis's first record on RCA, following his superb early work for Sun Records in Memphis; and it was his first hit —#1 for eight weeks in the spring of 1956. It is an amazing construct. The song was written by Mae Axton and Tommy Durden with the intention of coming up with a hit for Elvis; a

---

* Dan Hicks of the Charlatans

newspaper story about a suicide who'd left a note reading "I walk a lonely street" provided the specific inspiration. A song about a place that's actually an emotion is always a good idea. The lyrics are country clever and r&b quick. And the sound . . .

The power of the song is its ferocious intimacy, the closeness of Presley's voice to the ear and heart of the listener. That voice is penetrating and enveloping, and the song's arranger wasn't afraid to lead with his or her strongest card: the first line of the record is sung without accompaniment, punctuated at the end by two beats, two chords on the piano. Exquisite. This pattern is repeated through the verse, a cappella singing, piano crash, more a cappella singing; and then Elvis sings the chorus backed only by the beautiful, lonesome sound of a walking electric bass. The risk—only a great voice can hang out there that naked—is impressive; the payoff is phenomenal. At the end of the second chorus a guitar comes in, faintly; later the bass notes begin to be reinforced (I think) by an almost inaudible drumbeat. In the chorus after the third verse the bass is joined by a bit of tasty piano tinkling, and still the verse sound is as spare as ever—and then the fourth verse-and-chorus is followed by a remarkably dramatic instrumental break: a hard rock guitar solo, unmistakable, perhaps the first specific instance of the genre, slashing through the night and just as quickly replaced by a few hot lines from the piano to complete the break and bring us back to the closing verse. Wow.

None of which would matter, I suppose, if it weren't that the voice that this perfect and daring bit of accompaniment supports is nothing short of awesome. Spirit is walking throughout this recording. Just put it on the phonograph, and the room fills with ozone. Darkness and gloom drip joyfully from every rafter. This "Heartbreak Hotel" voice is an instant old friend; it intimately and unforgettably announces the arrival of something big.

*First release:* RCA 47-6420, January 1956

# 5 Little Willie John

## *Fever*

Here's one that happened to come out in the summer of '56, but it could have been any year, any moment. My eleven-year-old stepdaughter Heather just heard it and wants me to tape it for her. She thinks it'll be a good song to dance to. That says it all.

It *is* a good song to dance to. There's great power in its simple, luminous imagery, and an extraordinary grace in the sound of the performance. Peggy Lee ('58) and the McCoys ('65) did later versions of the song that are also very moving, which might suggest that the song's the thing, and it is, but though "Little" (eighteen years old) Willie John didn't write the song (credit goes to Johnny Davenport and Eddie Cooley), he did make it his own, and it is his performance as much as the written words and music that can be heard beneath and throughout the later, more popular versions. (More popular with white people—both the later versions were top 10 pop hits, while Willie's only got to #24; but there was a separate market for black music in '56 as there still is today, and on the "rhythm & blues" charts "Fever" by Little Willie John was a #1 record.)

"Fever" is a sensuous record, and as such it speaks powerfully to not only the stirrings but also the deep, pervasive *feelings* of sexuality in preadolescents and virginal adolescents (such as I was when I heard Little Willie John via the McCoys in 1965). Blues and rock and roll music both have great appeal to that part of us which cries out to be sexual even, or especially, when our bodies or emotions are not yet ready to go all the way. We listen to the music, sing or play it in our minds, and feel ourselves transubstantiated, projected into the act, entering into or being entered by the mystery. "You give me fever—" This is universal, waking up in a sweat, happily, fearfully possessed by desire. It is more than physical need. It's love. Willie John says it all when he shouts "Fever!" in the third line of the chorus, but "Bless my soul I love you/Take this heart away" is also a pretty good articulation of the spiritual arousal and abandon every one of us has felt. The church/bedroom connection again. A teenager might have almost no one to talk with about these feelings, but she or he can always play the record. Over and over.

All I know about Little Willie John is that he recorded a series of r&b hits for the King label between 1956 and 1960, and he died in prison in 1968 at the age of thirty. Perhaps he lies in an unmarked grave, but in my heart at least he has a tombstone, and on it is written, He gave us Fever.

*First release:* King 4935, May 1956

# 6 The Five Satins

## *In the Still of the Nite*

Still waters run deep. Rock and roll is a music of revealed truth, like all musics I suppose, and yet if this is so well understood then why is "professionalism" always held in such high regard? Maybe it's because we fail to distinguish between professionalism in the musician (it is indeed a good thing to show up at announced gigs) and in the music. In the music what can it be at best but imitation (practiced repetition) of revelation? The subject comes up because "In the Still of the Nite" is a thoroughly amateur record, one of those B-sides by an unknown teenage group on a tiny label that got turned over and became a national hit. And it is also a perfect jewel of revealed truth, an innocent intuitive masterwork.

Paul Simon in a song with a title too long to mention speaks of his characters secretly listening to "the Penguins, the Moonglows, the Orioles, the Five Satins—the deep forbidden music they'd been longing for." "In the Still of the Nite" (correct spelling) was written by Fred Parris on an army base in Philadelphia while on all-night guard duty. He recorded it with his band in the basement of a church in East Haven, Connecticut, just before the army sent him to Japan. He's thinking about (or pretending to think about; is there a difference?) a girl: "In the still/Of the nite/I held you/Held you tight/'Cause I love/Love you so/Promise I'll never/Let you go/In the still of the nite." The other four Satins create a mood (Parris's lead vocal is calm, detached, but set against the background voices, it comes across as achingly poignant) by repeating nonsense syllables over and over before and behind and around the lyrics: "shoo-doot, shoby do; shoo-doot, shoby do." Simple? You bet. But something happens. The word "night," always magical, combines with a certain harmonic resonance and the, um, melody, or maybe it's the song itself starts *vibrating*. . . .

At the end of each verse the nonsensical drone is interrupted: the background singers pause while the title is sung, and then echo it meaningfully. But the transcendent quality of the song is sparked, I believe, by a brilliant bit of business in the second verse, where the first words ("I remember") are immediately picked up by the background singers and turned into a "shoo-doot"-like repeating fabric, weaving around the other lyrics, pushing the already intense mood of quietude into a reverie of intimate nostalgia.

But this is nostalgia with a purpose: "I'll hope/And I'll pray/To keep (boom boom)/Your pre– (boom boom)/cious love." Immediately (no chorus, no pause) the melody goes back to what would be the beginning of a new verse—"Well before/The light/Hold me again/With all of your might"—but turns out to also be an extended lead-in to the chorus line ("In the still of the nite," followed by echo and then the instrumental/background vocal break). He doesn't just remember; he hopes and prays (the song is his prayer) to keep her love, until he returns from overseas or in other words forever and ever.

This is real; these feelings are what our lives are made up of. The power of this recording is its primitive, intelligent closeness to essence: essence of melody, harmony, musical structure, the essential expressiveness of the human voice. In such a mood of inspiration we try a few simple tricks (at the end: "In the still"—dramatic pause—"Of the nite," followed by a soaring, rising scale "oooh-weeee," brilliant vocal confection, to be heard again at some of the best moments in the careers of the Beatles, the Beach Boys, and the Who, among others). How music reveals feeling. How feeling, honestly expressed, conveys a deeper truth. How the desire to write, sing, play music becomes the fact itself, a bridge between strangers and across time. How innocent spontaneity becomes genius in hindsight. How the Indian drone and the repetitive Greek chorus emerge in the New World on inner city streets and leap to the airwaves. How deep forbidden music is made.

*First release:* Standord, August 1956

# 7 Bo Diddley

## Mona

Authority. According to the cliché, rock and roll is an expression of youthful revolt against adult authority, but that's a half-truth at best. The great rock and roll records go far beyond questioning or expressing dissatisfaction with the status quo; rather, they succeed in establishing a new authority all their own. Unselfconscious, these artists run out into unknown territory no one else even suspected existed, suss out the vibration of the place, and shout out, "Here I am!"

Bo Diddley arrived on the rock/r&b scene with a stunning double-sided proclamation of his own existence: "Bo Diddley" (the ultimate eponymous song title) backed with "I'm A Man." He borrowed from Muddy Waters, borrowed from Latin music, borrowed from urban Negro jivin' street humor (anticipating rap music by several decades)—like any good rocker he took a little from anything and everything that caught his attention or stuck in his mind, and mixed it up into something utterly and unforgettably his own. Bo Diddley's sound (not just a beat but a *sound,* indeed a whole complex of sounds) is the forceful, undeniable expression of a new reality loose in the world; and never more authoritative, more absolute, more self-contained or self-explanatory or self-fulfilling (apocalyptic; the moment has arrived; this is it) than on Bo's two-minute-and-eighteen-second epiphany (released in '57 as the B-side of the r&b hit "Hey! Bo Diddley") called "Mona."

To listen to "Mona" is to feel the universe shudder.

Like the African mask-faces of the women in Picasso's revolutionary painting "Les Demoiselles d'Avignon," the African moans that issue from Bo Diddley's mouth in "Mona" pierce the consciousness of the listener, the observer, demanding that he or she immediately recognize and acknowledge the incompleteness of Western consensual perception. There *are* deep emotional truths and archetypes whose existence we deny or belittle as we go through our daily motions of holding the world together. The moans in "Mona," and the shuddering rhythmic instrumental echoes of those moans, confront us inescapably with this potent, repressed information about who humans are and what happens in our lives. These truths cannot be spoken in existing language, and so the artist—in this case the performing artist—breaks open language by reaching for its antecedents, in the process inventing (rediscovering; seeming to invent) new ways of communicating, new ways to transfer visceral, felt truth from one human to another. The immediate impact on the listener of course is not the new techniques (those have impact over the next many decades, as other musicians try to re-create what they heard and felt from this recording) but the "new" (previously unacknowledged) truths. We hear them. We know them. We see through the transparent cement, the evanescent steel girders, of our twentieth-century reality, into the underlying rhythmic reality of the pulsing, organic universe we really live in. We moan in response.

"Hey! Hey, hey, Mona . . ." It's a song about desire, a song about turning to jelly. But, uh, dignified jelly, proud jelly, the kind that maintains its integrity no matter what. The suburban imagery of the lyrics ("Tell you Mona what I wanna do/Build a house next door to you./ . . . We can throw kisses through the blinds") is bizarre and comic up against the naked sexuality and irresistible power of the music, the rhythm, the voice. This is a man revealing the intensity of his feelings, pledging his love by frankly and beguilingly admitting his need. "Without your love I'd surely die." I mean, if you care about me at all, what more do you need to know?

There's a voodoo power in this recording, heavy primal magic. Not the image of magic, mind you; that wouldn't be enough to drive three generations and more of young musicians crazy with the desire to make music like this. No, actual magic. You can reach out and touch it. Or rather, you can put it on the phonograph, and wait confidently. *It* will reach out and touch *you.*

*First release:* Checker 860, May 1957

# 8 Jerry Lee Lewis

## *Whole Lot of Shakin' Going On*

"Mona" never made the pop Top 40 (none of Bo Diddley's records did, with the exception of his 1959 spoken-word novelty, "Say Man"). By contrast, Jerry Lee Lewis's equally revolutionary, equally authoritative "Whole Lot of Shakin' Going On" went to #3 on the pop charts in the summer of '57 (and was a #1 record in both the r&b and country markets). Such are the advantages of having white skin, no doubt. But also there is something about this recording that makes it quintessentially pop. Somehow—through sheer charisma, I think—Jerry Lee packages wild craziness and makes it feel safe. I don't mean that it *is* safe. This is a dangerous, out-there performance if there ever was one. But it's too cute, too charming, to really seem threatening (even if it was initially banned by BMI, the song-licensing organization). Indeed, "Whole Lot of Shakin' " is a testament to the power of charm, its ability to break down defenses and smuggle wild (sexual, musical, Dionysian) craziness into the homes and hearts of normal law-abiding citizens. "We ain't fakin'." You hear him say it, but you don't believe it —until it's much too late.

Jerry Lee Lewis, like Little Richard, had sex and God wrapped up tight like *that* in his early days as a musician, sure of himself and sure of God's power and also sure of the holy power of sexual attraction and expression—but damned unsure how the three fit together. When he thought about it, in fact, he couldn't put them together, except by defining himself as a hopeless (and regretful, if unrepentant) sinner. But when he made music, when he played for an audience, the three came together again like destiny incarnate. "Whole Lot of Shakin' " —not a song so much as a rave-up, a display of instrumental (and vocal) virtuosity—is as perfect a rock and roll record as one could hope to find, precisely because it draws from and fits into so many different American folk musics, and because it can move *any* listener from neutral to rockin' in seconds. It serves also as perfect illustration for one of my favorite passages from the ancient Chinese book of wisdom called the *I Ching:*

> When, at the beginning of summer, thunder—electrical energy—comes rushing forth from the earth again, and the first thunderstorm refreshes nature, a prolonged state of tension is resolved. Joy and relief make themselves felt. So too, music has power to ease tension within the heart and to loosen the grip of obscure emotions. The enthusiasm of the heart expresses itself involuntarily in a burst of song, in dance and rhythmic movement of the body. From immemorial times the inspiring effect of the invisible sound that moves all hearts, and draws them together, has mystified humankind.

Oh, those obscure emotions! Jerry Lee knows them as well as anyone, and so when he loosens their grip for himself, he does it for all of us. Ain't fakin'. Prophetic words. The greatest truths (by which I mean this entire performance, from start to finish) seem to exist as spontaneous bursts of selfness, of individual personality just breaking through, responding to our collective need, expressing it, relieving it, illuminating it. Bright piano. Bright guitar. Bright evil laugh. Bright mystery. Whole lot of shakin' going on.

*First release:* Sun 267, June 1957

# 9 Buddy Holly

## *Peggy Sue*

As if. As if communication were as simple as walking into a recording studio with a drummer, a guitar, and your voice, and then proceeding to speak in music. If you had Buddy Holly's voice, and mind, and charm, and self-belief, and integrity, and musical imagination, maybe you too could create a "Peggy Sue." A wild fantasy, to be sure, but what do you think McCartney and Lennon, Dylan, Jagger and Richards, Fogerty, Townshend, and the rest spent their teen years daydreaming about? They wanted to be rock and rollers: stand like Elvis, shout like Little Richard and Jerry Lee, rock like Chuck, testify like Muddy, and speak in music like Buddy Holly. Simplified, they just wanted to be Buddy Holly. Listen to "Peggy Sue" and you'll understand why.

Ease and power. The man's voice goes everywhere, not randomly but freely, with so much presence, so much awareness and intelligence, it's like an excited conversation with a close friend in which the way he's looking at you and the gestures he makes with his hands and eyes triple the information content of what he's saying. Except in this case it's all sound, as Buddy, not for the sake of art but just for the vital purpose of getting across to you (you alone) what he's feeling, invents a dozen new ways of using the human voice as a communicative vehicle, in the course of a single performance.

The song is hypnotic, not in the sense of simple repetition but in its unveiling of just how complex and varied seemingly simple repetition can be. The singer repeats the title (girl's name, also your name, since song is sung to "you") twenty-three times, with another six "Peggy"s thrown in for good measure. He says "I love you" eleven times, and manages eight "pretty"s in two quick bursts. In the most important progression, the last line of the first two verses follows "I love you gal" with "yes I love you"; this becomes "I love you gal and I need you" in the third verse, and then "I love you gal, I want you" in the fourth. With the mention of desire, the song breaks open: hunger can be heard in the vocal, the drums beat louder, and Buddy goes into his lead guitar break, which is entirely and unforgettably a celebration of wanting, with perhaps even a few hints as to the ways in which wanting ultimately finds expression. Intense. There are only two musicians on this recording, Holly and drummer Jerry Allison, but Crickets guitarist Nikki Sullivan was needed in the studio to switch the lever on Holly's guitar from bass (rhythm) to treble (lead) and back again. The fact that Holly and Allison make it sound so easy doesn't mean they weren't working their butts off.

And that's where the power comes in. A truly great artist is one who is able to make room for, indeed surrender to, the spontaneous, within a context of conscious intention and uncompromising determination (quiet, unyielding commitment to one's inner vision). So, according to legend, "Cindy Lou" became "Peggy Sue," at Allison's request (a tribute to his wife-to-be), and Holly's dissatisfaction in the studio with the sound of the song as a cha-cha led him to suggest that Allison try some paradiddles (drum rolls used by drummers when practicing) and lo, a new sound was created. The gains produced by these accidents or last-minute inspirations are immeasurable ("pretty-pretty-pretty-pretty Cindy Lou" doesn't cut it—got to have that popping labial for Buddy's voice to bounce off—besides, the similarities to Dale Hawkins's recent "Suzie-Q" would have been all too obvious), but at the same time no one listening to this performance can doubt that the finished song was there inside Holly from the beginning and that nothing (certainly not attachment to a particular beat or name) was going to keep him from realizing it.

There is something *perfect* about the sound of this song. It gets into the blood. Buddy Holly could have been a country singer, or pop crooner, could have and probably would have fitted his talent to whatever music was happening in the world when he came along. It happened to be rock and roll. But it only fully became rock and roll the day Buddy Holly started singing it.

*First release:* Coral 61885, September 1957

# 10 Danny and the Juniors

## At the Hop

Catchy tune. Attractive beat. The role of pop music since time immemorial has been to reach out and hook us via our well-known susceptibility to certain melodic and rhythmic configurations, and rock and roll certainly is pop music, whatever other pretensions writers like me may try to graft onto it. Oh yeah, and dumb words. The joyful, liberating power of a few well-chosen dumb words should never be underestimated.

"Let's go through the hop!" That's what I choose to hear, though he's clearly singing *"to* the hop" at least part of the time, and history tells us that the song was actually "Do the Bop" until the ever-sharp Dick Clark of American Bandstand (this is a *Philadelphia* record, and American Bandstand was a Philadelphia-based show) pointed out to the producer that the Bop (a local dance craze) was or soon would be on its way out, and suggested a lyric change. The idea was to keep the record current for a few more months, long enough to become a hit; thirty-odd years later you can still hear this song on the radio. The right dumb words (ask any advertiser) sure can make a difference.

But there's more to this record than cheerful stupidity. There's also great handfuls of our old friend, naive genius. That genius doesn't always have to originate with the performer (always, in rock legend, some eager kid off the streets; Voltaire's "noble savage"); it can just as well be the contribution of the producer (in rock legend the king-maker, the professional, the cynic, though in fact he may be just as hungry and just as wet behind the ears as the artist he's recording). Often it's a synergy of artist(s) and producer(s) working together—"At the Hop" was co-written by one of the guys in the group (not Danny) and a local producer, with additional credit going to the owner of the (tiny) record company who "conducted orchestra & chorus." Dick Clark, we know, stuck in his two cents' worth. And ultimately the end product has this breath of perfection about it, I mean there have been hundreds of thousands of records like this one, thousands of which have made the charts, scores of which have even also been #1 records, but very few with the magic, the enduring freshness, that breathes and frolics through every moment (all two minutes and thirty-one seconds) of "At the Hop."

The song makes you want to dance. It's got everything—humorous four-part doo-wop harmonies, a great jumping piano solo, cool earnest tongue-in-cheek lead vocals, deep-voiced "Oh baby"s, shouts of "Let's go!" kicking off the chorus, nonstop rhythmic underpinning, and one of the most graceful sudden endings ever recorded—and all in exactly the right places, never piled on too thick, nothing that comes across as slick or premeditated, just pure inspired God-given perfect timing and natural delight all the way through. Every element in place, and in motion. How's it done? You can take it apart and put it back together but you'll never really find out, never really be able to do it quite this way again, because the secret ingredient is grace.

Happy music. Rock and roll songs tend to be either about need ("Mona") or fulfillment ("Whole Lot of Shakin' Going On") or both at once. "All the cats and chicks can get their kicks at the hop." It's like a sign showing you where the immortal river is, and inviting you to jump in. Hey, right over here! Come on. Let's go. Through the hop.

*First release:* Singular 711, October 1957

# 11

## Chuck Berry

# *Johnny B. Goode*

History is still the enemy, and the danger is that if we talk about the pivotal role this record played in the ultimate triumph of the electric guitar as the symbol of rock music, talk about how more than any other this performance established the *sound* of the rock and roll guitar (as taught by Chuck's apostles: Carl, George, Keith, Jimi, Jimmy, et al.), talk even about the delightful fact that Voyager 1 is currently heading for the stars with a copy of "Johnny B. Goode" included in its two-hour recorded message in a bottle for whatever intelligent critters it may encounter, if we do any of this stuff, we risk further enshrining the song in its rock-and-roll-hall-of-fame, golden oldie, "classic rock" glass case, missing the one essential fact, which is that this record has something to offer far more important than its famous past or its imagined future—it exists now, a living presence in your ears, alive and available to be interacted with, to re-create itself via your phonograph, radio, boom box, CD player, a sound, a song, a human voice accompanied by slightly more-than-human musicians, the definition of a great record, an experience as rare and ordinary and rewarding as the sunrise, ladies and gentlemen, from deep down in Louisiana close to New Orleans, rock and roll's finest single fictional creation, Mister Johnny B. Goode.

Don't ask him any questions. Just listen.

The first thing you hear is six seconds of solo lead guitar (one drumbeat right in the middle), a repeating riff a little like the sound of the starter motor on a car, boom the drum signifies the engine kicking in, oh that feeling of power to go from stillness to mobility with a twist of the wrist and a push of the foot, riding the guitar chord, here we go, and the second thing you hear is the rest of the intro, full band (piano, bass, drums) and guitar rocking back and forth, building up potential energy, ready to explode, and then the vocal starts, zoom, steady acceleration, we're roaring down the road now, lyrics flowing like pure poetry ("never ever learned to read or write so well"), voice fierce relaxed free and gleeful, the verse being movement three and then it moves right into four, that incredible chorus, everything in the song so far has prepared you for this and yet nothing could prepare you for the way you find yourself reacting as Chuck sings, "Go! Go, Johnny, go!" and answers himself on the guitar, you're in the audience, you can see the kid playing, you're jumping out of your chair and hollering out "Go!" along with the singer, you and the stranger in front of you have your arms around each other and you're boogying, sweat pouring down your brow, but the band won't let up, piano raving away behind everything, and now they're into the second verse and chorus, movements three and four over again, erupting finally into a sequence almost too complex and too intense to keep track of, piano explodes for a second and then the guitar solo, the kid cutting loose, so assertive, so easy and powerful, clearly the announcement of some kind of new era, guitar then joined by piano and rhythm section, they're wailing together and reach a joyous climax and just when you think the third verse is about to start, look out, here comes another guitar solo and this time you're just totally lost, you become the guitar player, the country boy, grinning as the lightning dances out the ends of your fingers in time with the beat, totally liberated, the band comes in with a reprise of movement one, the third verse starts and you *are* Johnny B. Goode, and you're still the audience, and you're also somebody listening to this singer sing about the legendary musician and his audience, and it's just wonderful . . . If you actually listen to the words of the song, Johnny isn't a legend yet, may not even have a band yet except in his own imagination, he's fantasizing this just like we are ("strumming with the rhythm that the drivers made"). The true rock and roller, then, is not Johnny on stage but Johnny under the tree dreaming about being on stage, and the fire of that dream is what he takes with him to share when his moment does come. The sound of the guitar like the feeling of a car when you're joyriding it down the highway: listen, space critters, *this* is who we are.

*First release:* Chess 1691, March 1958

# 12 The Everly Brothers

## *All I Have to Do Is Dream*

It goes by so fast. But it won't go away. This song has been running through my head for years and years, and I don't even know why, just kind of got stuck in here somehow. It's so pretty, so evanescent, so—dreamlike. Richard Meltzer used to use the term "heaven rock" to describe certain songs, certain performances; to me it means a "lighter than air" sound, not lightweight but just the opposite—immensely powerful, monstrously forceful and affecting, precisely because of its unearthly, mysterious lightness. And therefore "rock," in the very subjective sense of "songs created in a rock context, in the rock era, that do in fact rock us to our foundations and thus help make life satisfying, exciting, worth living." Got that? Anyway, when my more linear mind asks me how I can listen to "All I Have to Do Is Dream" and call it rock and roll, I get momentarily defensive (yes I do, even though I know I'm right, and even though I know I don't have to justify anything), but then I notice that in the good year 1958 this record was #1 not only on the pop and country charts, but on the r&b charts as well. On the r&b charts?? Which just comes back to the same thing: some sounds are so white that they're not white at all, they zoom far beyond the bonds of this culture and its categories and preconceptions. Knock me over with a feather. With the suggestion of a feather. And the listener needs no justification or explanation. All he knows is, he loves the sound. It caresses his spirit. Sticks in his mind.

The message of the song is one eternally repeated by songwriters, and eternally appealing. It looks back to Leadbelly's "Goodnight Irene" ("I'll get you in my dreams") and ahead to the Temptations' "Just My Imagination" and to Jonathan Richman in 1971 anticipating both punk and the new age with the Modern Lovers' wonderful "Astral Plane":

Tonight I'm all alone in my room
I'll go insane

If you won't sleep with me I'll still be with you
I'm gonna meet you on the astral plane.

(Unless of course Leadbelly gets to you first.)

But back to the Everlys. They don't sound like two guys. But they don't sound like one guy, either. They sound (let's face it) like an angel. That vocal texture combined with this subject matter (dreaminess, impotence, desire as a possession, longing, precious pleasurable sweet sadness) is so remarkable, so mysterious, so immediately familiar, so penetrating . . . there is no way to communicate on paper (to someone who hasn't heard the performance) the semantic content of the words "I need you so that I could die" as sung here by these voices. And yet the meaning is unmistakable, inarguable, in the listening. The climax of the song for me is their reading of the five-word couplet—like a koan, a riddle at once obvious and infinitely challenging—"Only trouble is/Gee whiz." I'm not trying to be funny. I've thought of writing a book called *Only Trouble Is.* The phrase literally haunts me.

Notice that there is no instrumental break in this record; after the opening nonmelodic guitar chord (fascinating gesture, like a door closing, the end at the beginning) it's vocals straight through to the fade. The bridge occurs twice. Every phrase leads into another, and always that wonderful trembling reading of "dream," stretched out like a little musical bridge itself, five syllables, two "high tenors with about a third of a note's difference between their voices" (I read that somewhere), "dree-ee-ee-ee-eam," God I love it, it's just like some kind of a close friend, I don't even have to listen to the record with this one, it's just with me.

And then it's gone again. Who was that guy? How does he do that with his voice?

*First release:* Cadence 1348, March 1958

# 13 The Bell Notes

## *I've Had It*

Not a famous record for some reason, but unquestionably the best "la-la-la-la" in rock history, and that maracas opening ain't bad either. And the guitar is so sophisticated, so slyly funny, you'd swear it's Nick Lowe reaching back from 1979 to make the perfect archetypal rock and roll/pop single, borrow a little of everything (Buddy, Jerry Lee, doo-wop, and *lots* more) and put it all together with a slick, sassy charm too worldly, and too innocent, and too full of its own special personality, to ever be anything but authentic. Nice idea, but unless Nick had a time machine or secretly grew up on Long Island the Bell Notes beat him to it by a good twenty years. The record got to #6 on the national charts, the group was never heard from again, and the fact that the song hasn't been discovered by the "oldies" stations is just the icing on the cake. A gem, that's what it is. It has a freshness that will never fade, sounding better every time you play it, a record from some other planet, eternally outside of time.

The opening couplet is a masterpiece in itself:

When I saw her on the corner
Then I knew that I was a goner

and the thing is, a well-turned phrase takes on a life of its own in the ears of its listeners; and I've always (since 1959, anyway) tended to hear this as "then I knew that I wasn't gonna," pronounced "gonner" so we don't lose the exquisite near-rhyme, a phrase full of some kind of ineffable meaning for me. That is, obviously it doesn't mean anything, and it isn't even what he's really singing, but that doesn't matter; it's the way the song reaches us that counts. And the way it reaches us is more a matter of genius than of accident.

This is a funny song. The lyrics work because we identify with this guy as he (gently but mercilessly) laughs at himself for being such a victim. The music works because it is rock and roll laughing at itself, celebrating its own clichés. The celebration of clichés would later become a big part of '60's rock, with the Beatles leading the way. It's like, all pop songs have always been turned into big jokes at parties or in dormitories or locker rooms as we the listeners sing them to each other, mimicking all the most ridiculous and memorable parts—and rock and roll, as it has cannibalized itself over the years, starting very early, has had this great willingness to be aware of its own absurdity and lean into it more than a little. The bass player in the first instrumental break in "I've Had It" doesn't have to say, "Hey, let's boogie-woogie!" 'cause he knows we know he's kidding around here; and the hint of piano in the middle of the bit comes at just the right time to confirm that this song *is* every bit as intentionally silly (and therefore friendly and intelligent) as we thought it was all along.

And then the "la-la-la-la"s again. And the guitar! And the triply perfect ending. Sheer inspiration. Makes me smile. Every time. Can't ask for more than that.

*First release:* Time 1004, January 1959

# 14 Johnny and the Hurricanes

## *Crossfire*

When I was ten years old, I had a little plastic transistor radio (red and yellow) with an earphone, and I would go to sleep listening to it and sometimes take it to school. That was around the same time I discovered that the record store a mile from my house gave away free copies of the top 40 list from the local radio station, and I started riding my bike there every week to pick up the sheet as soon as it came in, filled with almost unbearable curiosity about what the new positions would be. Anyway, one night before I fell asleep, or maybe one day at recess, I heard an instrumental called "Crossfire" by Johnny and the Hurricanes, and it had a tremendous impact on me. I liked it, it made me excited, it had an energy and a resonance that was somehow very personally meaningful to me—it was my record, my sound (the fact that I discovered it on my own, before it was popular with the other kids, might have been a factor). I bought a copy. I listened to it over and over. I heard it in my head during the day's activities. I played it for my brothers. It was my theme, and being an instrumental especially it made me feel like I was in a movie and this was the soundtrack or part of the soundtrack. It made my life more dramatic, more romantic. I liked the way it made me feel about myself. I liked its hard-driving insistence. It gave me a feeling of power, a feeling that the universe I lived in was an exciting, awesome place.

Thirty years later, after playing it over and over enough times to wipe away any consideration of nostalgia, it still gives me the same feeling. I love the sound, the riff (actually three distinct riffs—the pervasive rhythmic one, the sax lead, and the charming guitar response). A good record has a sound—color, texture, personality—all its own, enriching our universe like the sound of a friend's voice, the way he or she talks that could only be that one person, if you've ever had a friend die you know how the sound of his voice stays in your mind, affirming the uniqueness of your loss and also of your gain in having known him at all. No one else's voice sounds like that, speaks to me like that, and in a real sense who I am is defined by the voices I know and recognize and love.

What I am getting at is that each record heard and felt and loved, embraced, actually expands, adds to, one's personal universe. If my cartographer were watching, he would have to add another mountain or canyon or meadow right over here that didn't exist before. I have grown. I have "Crossfire" pulsing through my veins now, its kinetic energy entertaining me and driving my life forward, and like a true friend I can't lose it, it will always be part of my consciousness.

Odd, though, that it is also a physical object, a seven-inch circle of plastic with a big hole in the middle. Hello, old acquaintance. Despite all we've shared together, I feel certain I could meet you today for the first time and recognize you just as clearly. Just like when I was ten, I'd say, wow, I've been waiting all my life to hear this. Your kineticism, your rhythms and melodies and the grittiness of your saxophone voice, tell me something I never knew before (and will never forget again) about who I am.

*First release:* Warwick 502, April 1959

# 15 Chuck Berry

## *Memphis, Tennessee*

In June 1959 Chuck Berry released a single called "Back in the U.S.A.," with the tag line "I'm so glad I'm livin' in the U.S.A." Six months later the U.S.A. returned the favor by arresting and convicting him on trumped-up charges. His real crime was being black and successful (and insufficiently cautious) in a white society, so (poetic injustice) he was railroaded on a slavery statute, charged with involuntary servitude for providing transportation and a job at his nightclub to a young woman he met while performing. No coercion was involved, and I've never heard of a white musician being convicted of any similar charge. He served twenty months in federal prison—you can read the full story in his excellent autobiography.

The flip side of "Back in the U.S.A." was a song called "Memphis, Tennessee." According to Berry, this was recorded at his office in St. Louis "in the heat of a muggy July afternoon with a seventy-nine-dollar reel-to-reel Sears, Roebuck recorder . . . I played the guitar and the bass track, and I added the ticky-tick drums that trot along in the background which sound so good to me." The song was not a hit in its original form, but in 1963 Lonnie Mack put out an instrumental version (just called "Memphis") that got to #5, and a year later Johnny Rivers hit #2 with a live, vocal version of the song. The rhythmic figure supporting Chuck's sweet vocals and sweeter slide guitar on the homemade original (two beats repeated four times, rising twice and then descending) was picked up by hundreds of other musicians; I don't know if Berry originated it, but it is still known to music-makers as the "Memphis" beat—you can hear it, for example, on Marvin Gaye's "Can I Get A Witness" (released five months after Lonnie Mack's hit) and on the Everly Brothers' delightful "Gone Gone Gone." The great-great-grandchildren of this rhythmic figure will still be shuffling their way through the folk and popular musics of a thousand nations long after you and I are no longer around to listen.

A good poet almost unthinkingly gives voice to the primary concerns of his or her era (long before they're identified by anyone else), so it is not surprising that Chuck Berry in 1958 penned this poignant story of father/daughter separation, though he himself was not divorced (and had never lived in Memphis). Once again he has crafted a brilliant fiction, stunning in its soft-spoken simplicity, its mythic power, and the oh-so-satisfying deadpan shocker in its next-to-last line. Not many rock and roll artists can raise goose bumps with their narrative skills. Berry also has the novelist's or poet's gift for language ("Last time I saw Marie she's wavin' me goodbye/With hurry-home drops on her cheek that trickle from her eye") and structure (notice how the words "help me" occur in each of the first three verses; the fourth marks the only appearance—at precisely the climactic moment—of "please") and most of all meter. He is an American poet laureate due particularly to his ability to uncover and articulate (the latter a performer's art; definitely a large part of good poeting) the hidden rhythms of the American vocabulary: "long *dis*tance infor*ma*tion" and *"Mem*phis, Tennes*see."* Then there's aptness of imagery and economy of storytelling ("my uncle took the message and he wrote it on the wall").

So he has the words, the rhythm, the story, the sound, and the music. He also has the voice, and the guitar. Small wonder we so revere our Uncle Chuck. A good looker, too—small wonder the feds were jealous. But a record like "Memphis, Tennessee" (and mark you well, there *is* no other record like "Memphis, Tennessee") transcends its component parts, transcends even its creator's talents. Its triumph is its smallness, its humanness. The quiet yelping of the guitar during the instrumental break, the magical sound made by bass and drums as they transition back to the verse, are as exciting in their own way as the orgiastic guitar solos of "Johnny B. Goode." Here is the human heart uncovering itself, sharing itself, writing its yearning message on the wall. "Call Marie." Okay, uncle, we will.

*First release:* Chess 1729, June 1959

# 16 Del Shannon

## *Runaway*

"As I walk along, I wonder . . ." I wonder a lot of things, for instance what ancient spirit was whispering in Del Shannon's ear the night he wrote the words to this song, pouring out one archetypal image after another, neatly disguised as banal teenage pop song lyrics, little phrases that stick to our mind-bones like oatmeal's supposed to do to our ribs: "what went wrong"; "while our hearts were young" (delicious to hear in this twenty-one-year-old voice, have we ever missed our youth as much as we did at that age?); "walking in the rain"; "tears are falling" "end this misery" . . . remarkable sweet mystery, the power of these particular words sung by this voice, accompanied by this music. You can break the performance down into a dozen or more component parts and each one—the organ solo, the falsetto warble ("wa-wa-wa-wa-wonder"), the nervous charming staccato beat, the melodic power of the final repeating phrase ("My little runaway, uh-run-run-run-run runaway")—seems a product of pure inspiration, single-handedly responsible for the song's magic, its success. Where do such marvels come from?

I don't like to dwell too much on "the stories behind the songs," the world these days seems all too eager to reduce everything to journalism and gossip, but this tale's a revealing one: a kid named Charles Westover is working in a carpet store in Michigan and fronting a band in a local bar; black deejay from another town comes to see him, likes him, introduces him to a couple of record company guys in Detroit (same ones who signed up those Toledo boys, Johnny and the Hurricanes), they sign him and send him to NYC to record some songs, call him in Battle Creek to tell him the stuff's too slow, come up with something peppier. Del (he's changed his name) recalls, "I wrote 'Runaway' on stage, at the Hi-Lo Club. I just kind of came up with it. Max Crook, my organ player, sat at the organ one night and he played A-minor, G, and I said, 'I never heard such a great change as that!' I proceeded to play the intro, and went right on with the structure of the song, and the next day I wrote the words." That night they taped it—Del says, "I told Max, 'When I point to you, play an instrumental,' and he played the instrumental that's on the record."

(That instrument he's playing, by the way, is a musitron—some kind of variation on the electric organ, an early incarnation of synthesizer. More gossip: Shannon says the runaway he was originally thinking about, before he changed the words around a little, was himself.)

Okay, so here's my theory. All of us are walking down the street every day and people are playing these A-minor, G chord changes and other marvels and we don't even notice, because we're not in that state of mind that says, "This is the moment, this is my one big shot to get out of the carpet store and do something interesting," or else we don't have the other half of it, the modesty that says, "I have no idea how I'm going to do this, but maybe I'll come up with something," that allows us to notice and accept and receive what the universe gives us. Likewise we're all sitting here with one fabulous little instrumental break ready to fly out our fingers, only we don't realize it's anything anyone would want to hear, and no one says to us, "Okay, tape's running, when I point to you, invent!" And then once in a very great while they do, and we're in a space to respond, and bang!: miracles. The inspiration's there all around us all the time, and yet when you consider the obstacles we put up to receiving it (including trying to get it, the greatest obstacle of all), it's no surprise that a record like "Runaway" doesn't come along very often.

And when we respond to this beauty, and it is indeed a fabulous young and brash yet anciently wise beauty we hear on this record, including, of course, the boyish joy in Shannon's voice because he knows (without necessarily expecting anything) how good this song he's written is—when we respond to it, I believe we are responding to our own memories of similar experiences, similar moments of inspiration, unexpressed perhaps but also unforgotten. We listen to the music, and remember.

*First release:* Big Top 3067, February 1961

# 17 Ben E. King

## *Stand By Me*

When a record is a big current hit and you hear it on the radio all the time it starts sounding bloated, overdone, overfamiliar, too famous and full of itself; contrariwise, the same record after it slips into obscurity can, when heard again, sound incredibly fresh, pure, simple, a breath of fresh air out of some unknown and intriguing past era. "Stand By Me," a top 10 hit for Ben E. King (former lead singer of the Drifters) in 1961, resurfaced twenty-five years later as the title song of a popular film (about, appropriately, coming of age circa 1960) and (a rare if not unique occurrence in the U.S.) became a top ten hit again, same artist, same recording. It also spurred the sale of some five million copies of the soundtrack album, insinuating itself into more ears and lives than it ever touched the first time. My (then) thirteen-year-old son bought a copy. Come 2011 and we could see the whole cycle repeated again, because this is an absolutely timeless recording, superficially corny (the strings) the moment it came out but built around a sound (the bass guitar and percussion and the sound of the space that encloses them and marries them to King's voice) and a vocal performance that cut immediately to the core of the listener's being.

What we have here, in effect, is the Twenty-third Psalm disguised as a love song. This is communicated not primarily by the words but by the way the words are sung, the timbre and tone of King's voice, the images he conjures up as he shapes each consonant, each vowel, each note. "No I won't be afraid" —this is sung to a lover ("Darling, darling" secularizes it forcefully, unambiguously; no one ever calls the Lord "darling"), but what comes across unmistakably (not consciously or overtly, of course; that would spoil the whole thing) is "Yea though I walk through the valley of the shadow of death, I will fear no evil, for Thou art with me."

"If the sky that we look upon/Should tumble and fall . . ."

and as I say it's the richness of the voice and the humility and dignity it expresses that matter here, along with a remarkable understated yet unstoppable rhythmic force that gives the verse the sweep of a Cecil B. DeMille biblical epic. The listener doesn't necessarily think about God. He or she thinks about friendship, about a warm fire on a cold, windy night, about love as a source of courage. At the end of the song, which is about a man pleading for and thus acknowledging (with dignity and affection) his lover's support, there's a surprising turnaround (more cosmetic language so we don't have to confront the deeply spiritual nature of the feelings the song evokes in us) as King tosses off "Whenever you're in trouble won't you stand by me," as if all along he's really been offering help rather than nakedly sharing his vulnerability and need. And it works. Each bit of redirection, each reassurance that this is just a pop song now and no longer the gospel standard it was adapted from, only seems to strengthen the song's underlying power, its message that, in fact, there is a higher power that stands behind your love and mine, strong enough to keep us safe and feeling safe even if sky and mountains and all material reality should fail.

Leiber and Stoller, the great songwriter/producer team, with some suggestions from their young protegé Phil Spector, produced "Stand By Me," and as the setting lets us appreciate the jewel, so the production and orchestration of this record are what allow us access to its incomparable vocal performance. Intimacy is the word. In the 1986 movie the song refers to the friendship between the preadolescent protagonists and, more specifically, the narrator's feelings as he discovers a greater depth and trustworthiness in himself than he previously imagined possible. As a hit in 1961, the song is about a love affair, you and me against the world. Either way—or in any of the many other ways the song can be taken—it is the intimacy the performance evokes (and creates) that gives it its power.

So maybe we don't want to share this intimacy with all these millions of other people who think they own this record. It's okay. There's no need to share. Let them all go. Turn down the lights, turn up the phonograph, and listen. The man is singing for you, and you alone.

*First release:* Atco 6194, April 1961

# 18 The Miracles

## *I'll Try Something New*

This one is really exciting. Part of it, for me, is the knowledge that I may have the privilege of introducing it to you; it only got to #39 on the pop charts when it came out in 1962, and isn't included on a 1985 compact disc called *The Greatest Songs Written by Smokey Robinson.* Yet it's a masterwork, equal to or perhaps better than Robinson's most famous records ("You've Really Got A Hold on Me," "The Tracks of My Tears"), and more illustrative of the full reach of the man's genius as a composer, lyricist, arranger, and vocalist. "I'll Try Something New" is as elegant and durable a bit of songwriting, and as expressive of its musical era, as "Mountain Greenery" or "God Bless the Child."

It's a ballad; what makes it a rock and roll ballad, if you will, is that, like Buddy Holly's exquisite "I Guess It Doesn't Matter Any More" (written by Paul Anka) or The Beatles' "Hey Jude," it is written and performed for a rock and roll audience (no way Smokey or his boss Berry Gordy were going to limit themselves to the black/r&b market once "Shop Around" hit it big), and it makes generous use of rock and roll's tradition of eclecticism and (as the title suggests) innovation. Smokey tries not one but dozens of new things in the course of this song, this recording, this performance; it is exciting to know that some of his innovations still haven't sunk in, still wait in the grooves of this record to influence and inspire future generations of musicians, composers, singers, writers, lovers.

Where to begin? The science fantasy imagery in these lover's promises is marvelous, a triumph of the imagination (as entertaining as the best fairy tales) and also perfectly suited to the persona of the singer, the rapturously enthusiastic, confident, intoxicated lover, probably more in love with the idea and feeling of love (the giddiness, the sense of power) than with the girl herself. The song is grandly romantic and mysteriously detached from romance at the same time (Robinson's trademark detachment, always asserting that things are not as they seem, and that what I assert, not what you perceive, is what's so).

The rhythm of the language, written and performed, triples or quadruples the impact of its content. And that's just the start, because in addition to his gift for rhythmic phrasing, Smokey has an extraordinary ability to add to and shift the meaning of a song's lyrics by changing the pitch of his voice. Melodies mutate from line to line, building on themselves and constantly creating new emphases in the song's narrative, new sound textures, new emotional implications. *Every* time he sings the title phrase it's different—in melody, in tone, in emphasis, and, subtly, in meaning. The climax, appropriately but surprisingly, comes in the last word of the song, a gorgeous ascending "new-oo-oo-oo-oo-oooh."

This is arrived at via a slick structural stunt. The verses themselves are ornate, far more subtle structurally than the ABAB CCDD rhyme pattern would suggest, but they do follow a familiar song form until the end of the third verse, when instead of just repeating the chorus (last two lines of the verse) and fading, Smokey repeats the melody of the two lines with new words, new images, and then does it again, and finally double-times a playful fourth couplet ("If at first I don't succeed try again is what I'll do . . ."), overwhelming and delighting the listener, who is set up to expect some repetition somewhere.

The harplike flourishes at the beginning are magically evocative and rich in humor; the strings at the end of the instrumental break are quietly, poundingly rhythmic, wonderfully effective; and how about that "Hey Venus!" from the backup singers, a nod to Frankie Avalon's hit of three years earlier? This is sophisticated stuff. And its complexity adds up to such pureness, such seeming simplicity, two and a half minutes of visionary raving (musical and lyrical) so calm and sweet you don't realize till days after you hear it how deep it's sunk its hooks in you. "On the moon above I'll write 'it's you that I love' . . ."

*First release:* Tamla 54059, May 1962

# 19 The Duprees

## *You Belong to Me*

One of the jobs of music is to evoke the textures of moments gone by, to bring back to us some part of who we were and what we felt at other times than now. Any piece of music can play this role; what is striking about "You Belong to Me" is that it is inherently nostalgic—it evokes a sense of the past the first time one hears it. The ultimate oldie. It sounded old the day it was released, just as "I'll Try Something New" sounds new even after twenty-seven years. Like Gray's "Elegy Written in A Country Churchyard" or Hardy's "The Darkling Thrush," it evokes (musically, not lyrically) the ending of an era, a mood of sadness, loss, foreboding, and acceptance. Fin de siècle. It celebrates the beauty of the old music, urging the singers to lift their voices for one last glorious chord, stretched out over the infinite, bursting with heartbreak, affection, redemption. Great ending. And an equally great beginning, mysterious (unless you're paying attention, and sometimes it's better not to, not to listen too close to the words—just let those images wash over you) and so evocative: "See the pyramids along the Nile." I see them. I feel the love in the singer's voice, and the sand beneath his sweetheart's feet, and I'm falling dreamlike into another world.

Life is loss. Of course, this is just a rather old-fashioned song (but *doo-wop* old-fashioned, rock and roll sensibilities, teen culture—not at all "easy listening" or "middle of the road"; I mean, our whole identities can depend on such subtle distinctions) in which a guy asks his girl to stay true to him. It isn't sad; rather heartwarming, in fact. The guy is caring without being obsessive, shares his vulnerability without whining or groveling, and certainly isn't carrying on as though he's already lost her (not like Bob Dylan in "Boots of Spanish Leather"). I'm not saying it's a song about loss. I'm saying the sound of the record, the sweet perfection of its background harmonies, its orchestration, its lyrics, its openmouthed lead vocal, somehow remind this listener in an oddly reassuring way of everything in his life that's gone and behind him and won't be seen again.

And I'm saying we love such reminders. They nourish us. They even, in a very subtle way, urge us to love the present moment, with all its challenges and awkwardness and disappointments, because someday it, too, will be the precious, unreachable, warmly remembered time gone by. Music! Music tells us as almost no other medium can that we actually existed in that other era, that there is some kind of continuity between then and now.

We keep losing our lives. We keep letting them go. Nothing belongs to us; everything is ultimately repossessed by time itself, whether we make our payments punctually or not. And it's all right. But sometimes we like to look the system in the eye, and get a little sentimental about the whole process, and at those moments music is our most reliable companion.

I don't know where these Duprees came from or where they went, but I like them. I like their voices; I like the feeling I get when I hear them sing this song. Maybe they just know what chords to sing to me in. Or maybe they know all the lost truths about time and space, and this was the only way they could put what they know into a language I'd understand.

*First release:* Coed 569, July 1962

# 20 The Beatles

## *Please Please Me*

Start over. Follow these simple instructions. Get a set of headphones and a sound system with some kind of decent amplifier, and a copy of "Please Please Me" (album, single, cassette, CD, whatever you can find. If you don't have it, knock on the two or three doors closest to your domicile, you'll come up with a copy, guaranteed). Turn off the speakers and listen to the song on headphones a couple of times. Then turn up the volume as high as you think you can bear and listen to it a few more times.

Keep going. Louder. Crank that sucker up. Push your limits.

Louder. Come on, you could be saving yourself thousands of dollars of psychotherapy here. Louder! That's it. Over the top. Breakthrough. Bliss. Release. Your heart is pounding, your bones are vibrating, your spirit wants to push away the walls of the world and scream to the far galaxies. "Come on (*come on*), Come on (*come on*), Come on (*come on*), Come on (*COME ON!*)"—I swear to God, it's like I never heard this record before, never really understood what the Beatles were all about until this evening. It's not that I haven't gone this far, but I guess I was just too proud to let those absurdly popular, universally palatable Beatles be the ones to bring me here.

I was a fool. This record is as tough and as revolutionary as anything any punk or heavy metallist ever attempted. It could kill you. It could set you free.

There's a story (which I believe) that when the Beatles were nobodies freshly arrived in Hamburg, being jerked around by the owner of some low dive where they were playing, John Lennon became so frustrated he stamped his foot on the stage while performing, trying to destroy it, venting his wrath (at God, as much as anyone), and the audience took it as part of the act, loved it, noticed the boys for the first time, required them to stamp through every song, every night, turned them into local celebrities.

The beat. We are (be truthful, now) unhappy with our lot, much of the time, and our unexpressed rage (at matters small and large) chokes our aliveness, cuts us off from love and joy and spontaneity and the sunshine on the hilltops. Noise comes in at us all the time, direct and indirect, including a whole new order of noise in this industrial vehicular electronic age, and we goddamn well need to give it back sometimes. And the beat's the answer, our salvation, our expression, our grounding device. Make it big. Lay it on thick. Look at what can be jammed into a single record, one minute and fifty-eight seconds! The Beatles came at the problem with a different perspective than Phil Spector, who was making major progress in beat-enlargement on his side of the Atlantic. Spector knew the studio, took charge of it, re-created it to his own specifications, mind over matter, the genius. The Beatles knew nothing, didn't care to know (not yet). Instead, they (John in particular) got an intuition of what they wanted, a glimmering, a whiff, and lunged for it, demanding it to be theirs. Nothing would stand in their way, they were too young and hungry and adrenaline-crazed to be denied. Two-track recording? Great! We'll mix it down to one track and pound through it again, sound on sound, louder, harder, fatter. Horn section? I'll do it on the harmonica. Harmonies? Okay, everybody sing at once now. Rhythm? Play the dirtiest bass line you can think of. Ringo can handle the rest on the drums. Wham! Wham! Wham!

Spirit over matter. Mind hardly enters into it. You just reach out for the possible and trust your inspiration, trust your medium, let loose your stampeding energies and don't look back. Say anything that comes into your mind. Bitch about your sexual hang-ups with the missus. It doesn't matter. They'll hear it as a love song.

Or a call to arms. "If I had my way," says Rev. Gary Davis. "If I had my way, in this wicked world. If I had my way, I would tear this building down." The Beatles smiled while they said it, and the world was theirs. They harmonized, with a vengeance. They rock and rolled. They kicked ass. They started something.

*First release:* Parlophone R 4983 (U.K.), January 1963

# 21 The Jaynetts

## *Sally Go 'Round the Roses*

It will be apparent to the reader by now, if it wasn't from the start, that my list of the 100 best rock and roll singles is not your list. Couldn't be. There are a lot of obvious reasons we could both name why this is so, but the essential reason may not be quite so obvious: they can't be the same because what makes a song, a record, a performance great is what it says about the person listening to it. That is, its greatness lies in the fact that it is so powerful, so transcendent, it actually speaks for the listener; I can, in a certain sense, define myself by the music I listen to. And I do. And so do you. And while our tastes may overlap (frequently, I hope), we are still very different people, each one of us distinct and different from everyone else. A great record reminds us of this, strengthens the listener's awareness of who he or she is, and the tremendous value of being exactly this person, no one else, no matter what.

A hit like "Sally Go 'Round the Roses" offers a neat paradox: it made it to #2 on the national charts in the U.S. precisely because (I suggest) it is so individualistic, so weird, that each listener who responds to it takes it as something very special and uniquely hers/his. Something other people probably wouldn't understand. Something that is precious to me, and speaks well of me, because I have the ability to appreciate and love it. Each of us feeling this, embracing it, buying it, putting it atop the charts, still feeling (quite rightly) that someone like me who can relate to "Sally Go 'Round the Roses" is one in a million.

True, to a certain degree, of every record in this book. Jumps out of the radio and speaks to me alone. "Roses they can't hurt you." Yeah. Tell it like it is, sister.

That piano riff. The organ when it comes in. The relationship between the voices, the rising and falling volume, the hypnotic, intense, circular, unfailing rhythm. It's just about as quintessential a rock single as there could be. You don't know where it came from or who these people are, and you don't want to know. Don't break the spell. Leave the magic circle unspoiled for the next person who may walk through these woods.

"Sally go 'round the roses. Sally go 'round the roses." Like a nursery rhyme. Scholars tell us that "ashes, ashes, all fall down" originated as a reference to the Black Plague. True or not, there is a jungle grapevine among us humans that is entirely separate from newspapers and universities. We find ways of passing on the truth. (Incidentally, a mixture of apple cider vinegar and garlic is rumored to have protected those who drank it regularly from falling to the Plague. Might be useful information someday.)

"Sally don't you go, don't you go downtown." So it's about seeing your boyfriend with another girl, but it just could be about Hiroshima, could be about almost anything too real and important to be spoken of in some less immediate context. Jump rope verses, hopscotch chants. The sound of this record. It's far beyond some kind of cleverness of the arranger or producer. For whatever reason, call it accident, there's an honesty to it, an integrity, an accuracy, that I at least can't fail to hear and feel.

And I happen to know I'm not alone.

*First release:* Tuff 369, June 1963

# 22 The Kingsmen

## *Louie Louie*

Sing swap grows blim blam fleegle, den possumcup hoppy potato pancake. Aftermumps, slackjaw fleegle den slalom inda mogsteroon, but not riffen or raffen exempt fleedermouse (dream baba dream baba dream).

A very long time ago, in a land considerably to the west of the Delaware River, there lived three passably talented musicians known as the Kingsmen. One night as they were walking home to their cold water triplex after many hours of playing "What'd I Say" and "Peggy Sue" and "Who Wears Short Shorts?" to seven or eight disinterested customers at Fernando's Pink Tulip Roadhouse, a Fairy Godmother appeared to them. Each Kingsman was granted a wish. One wanted to make a hit record. Another asked for wealth, fame, and plenty of sex. The third, who was drunker than the others, wished to create a great and enduring work of art that would communicate to all the world, including future generations, the existential essence of the evening they'd just spent on the bandstand at Fernando's. And so it came to pass.

Dream baba fleegle—no, no, enough of that. "Louie Louie" is a very famous record. The song was actually written by a black man named Richard Berry, who had a minor r&b hit with it in 1956. (He borrowed the dominant rhythmic figure from a Mexican song, supposedly "El Loco Cha Cha Cha.") Years later a white guy in Seattle, Washington, who played in a local band discovered the single (according to legend) in the bargain bin of a record store (very important truth about the single: it is an object, a fairly indestructible piece of plastic, and it has the ability to endure as a physical object even when the performance and song impressed on it are long forgotten).

The guy in Seattle liked the song and included it in his standard repertoire; eventually he joined a group that made a record, and that first garage band recording of "Louie Louie" (by the Wailers) became a regional hit in the Pacific Northwest.

The song was easy to play and easy to dance to, and it became part of the standard playlist of quite a few Northwest bands. One of those bands was the Kingsmen. They made a record of their version at a small Portland, Oregon, recording studio with highly primitive acoustics. Nothing happened for five or six months and then a copy of the object wandered into the hands of a Boston deejay, and the record became a national hit. And more or less from that day forward "Louie Louie" has been the international anthem of local bands (high school or college or dropout rock and roll bands, playing parties, bars, dances—not bands people look at, bands people *dance to*), surely the rock song that has been performed the most, at the grass roots level, every year since the Kingsmen first introduced it to the world.

So it's a famous record. (Its fame also derives from an intense controversy about "dirty lyrics"—the song was investigated by the FCC and even the FBI, without result—the point being that if you slur the vocals enough, whether through vocal technique or recording methodology or both, people will be able to hear in the song's lyrics whatever they want to hear.) A very influential record. But is it really one of the 100 best rock and roll singles, in terms of direct reward, listening pleasure, and like that? Yeah. I think so. It is.

Why? Well, see, it's the attitude. And the persistence of the rhythm and the crude clarity of the sound and the sloppy, undeniable fluidity of the guitar solo and the way the singer says "Okay, let's give it to 'em, right now!", all of which of course are simply the component parts, the external form, of the song's attitude. Beatitude. Like a Buddhist chant, one size fits all—no need for lots of different words or forms to entertain and impress the mind when the point is to lose and let go of your mind in the chant, the dance, the thrust of the sound. Let's say there's a precise right timing that triggers the essential experience of hearing and moving to rock and roll. Maybe the right attitude puts a musician in touch with the timing, maybe the timing and the attitude are one, a certain angle of incidence, who cares? The Kingsmen stumbled onto it. Oh, baby. We gotta go. Uh uh. Fairy Godmothers rule. Right now.

*First release:* Jerden 712, June 1963

# 23 The Beach Boys

## *Fun, Fun, Fun*

Always another wave coming along. Innocent and arrogant, the Beach Boys and the Beatles reinvented rock and roll (it had lost its identity between 1959 and 1962, a long, potentially deadly hiatus for a musical form that only became self-aware in 1955).

"Fun, Fun, Fun" starts by borrowing outright Chuck Berry's guitar intro from "Johnny B. Goode," a tribute as much as a rip-off. "Let your colors fly," the Beach Boys sang in their previous hit "Be True to Your School," and this purloined intro is just that, their pledge of allegiance to rock and roll and to the teenage nation for which it stands, with liberty (in the sense of unselfconscious freedom) and good times for all.

If Elvis hadn't been drafted, if Buddy Holly hadn't died, if the payola scandal hadn't weakened the independent labels and stations and strengthened the corporate, conservative side of the music biz, maybe "rock and roll" would have grown up (and vanished) with the generation that discovered it. Instead, the subteens who grew up listening to the stuff got to reenact the rock revolution and make it their own. Second generation. A new teen nation replaces the old one. Play a few notes of the old guitar anthem to establish our legitimacy (and celebrate our roots), and let's get on with the party.

By defining rock and roll as a wide-open playground to be reinvaded by each new generation of teenagers, the Beach Boys and the Beatles (paradoxically) consolidated the gains of the previous rock era, establishing rock as a renewable resource, an ongoing, vital, enduring creative form. This is the permanent revolution that Jefferson and Marx could only dream of; and apparently it will last as long as successive "generations" of Western teenagers have lots of money to spend on music and few responsibilities to distract them.

"Fun, Fun, Fun" is a teen vignette in the Chuck Berry tradition, and stands as one of the all-time classics of the genre.

Mike Love is underrated as a lyricist—"Well she got her daddy's car and she cruised through the hamburger stand now/ Seems she forgot all about the library like she told her old man now"—now admit it, that's inspired. Brian Wilson's legendary inventiveness comes into play in the second and third verses, with the Greek chorus echoing each line ("you shouldn'ta lied now, you shouldn'ta lied"). Notice that the rebellious, fun-loving, fast-driving hero of the song is female. Notice that in every verse, every line except the last ends in "now," and it works! (One of the jobs of poetry is to capture not the actual words but the subjective impact of everyday speech.) Notice the understated, very specific, rhythmic sound of the words "fun, fun, fun" in the chorus, and the contrasting open-endedness of "away." Notice the easy, natural, wildly complex interplay between the voices and combinations of voices. Notice the neat double meaning in the second verse, "A lot of guys try to catch her," referring both to her elusive sexuality ("you look like an ace now") and her automotive ability ("you drive like an ace now"). Notice how Dad's futile attempt at discipline only serves to throw her (potentially) into "my" realm and bigger and better trouble. And I know you can't fail to notice one of the sweetest fade-outs ever, the brilliant ordinariness of the song totally transcended in two brief moments of soaring falsetto. Fun, indeed.

Innocence and arrogance. It's a delicate combination, and you can't fake any part of it. Get it just right, and the world will retaliate by throwing money and love and praise at you till they finally knock you off balance. But they can't take away the warmth of the sun and the spirit of independence that radiate from the grooves of this permanently revolving recording.

*First release:* Capitol 5118, January 1964

# 24 The Beach Boys

## I Get Around/ Don't Worry Baby

At a certain level of intensity there is a complete lack of artifice. "Don't Worry Baby" is one of the pinnacles of rock and roll artistry because of its utter unselfconsciousness, its innocent, unmatchable power and sincerity. "Well, it's been building up inside of me for oh I don't know how long . . ." This first line is self-referential; it describes the music we're hearing, the feelings that are being shared. What's been building up is the speaker's need to confess his anxiety to the listener. Intuitively, the listener knows that the singer/writer/producer (Brian Wilson) is speaking directly to him, to the person on the other end of the recording process. Brian's courage in sharing his "irrational" fears so honestly, so directly, is extremely affecting. "I don't know why but I keep thinking something's bound to go wrong." It is the power of his relationship with us that frightens him; yet he holds back none of that power here. The singer is totally present with his fears, naked before us, and his honesty is liberating; it gives the listener permission to be in touch with his (her) own anxieties, if my hero has them it's okay that I have them too. Having set this up, the song can go about its business, which is a) direct reassurance, and b) celebration of the female, the lover/mother, as the sole power that can (for the male) disperse the anxiety, make it bearable, allow me to face the world, keep breathing, go on with my work.

The rest of the lyrics, placing these feelings in the context of an impending car race, are awkward; their purpose is to put a fig leaf over the song's unprecedented intimacy, thus allowing it to be performed, released, listened to. And the awkwardness doesn't matter, because all we need to hear are those opening lines and the three words of the title; everything else is layers of sound—primarily vocal (lead and harmonies) but there are extraordinary instrumental (percussive) inventions here, too—so human and real and unspeakably beautiful that one sinks into them as into a cloudbank of heavenly reassurance, safety, harmony, love, surrendering all care, transported by the fullness and grace of these incomparable melodic and sonic textures.

These voices. Our awe at Brian's courage, musical imagination, and creative power should not cause us to overlook the importance of his constant inspiration and primary tool: the sound of these harmonizing voices, never more exquisite or personal than in the first few seconds of "Don't Worry Baby," like the comfort found walking by the edge of the ocean, waves breaking on our shore, invaluable natural resource.

"I Get Around," other side of the record and the Beach Boys' first #1 hit, is also a masterpiece. Two for the price of one. And the closer one listens, the more awe-inspiring it is. It's like the forerunner of some major new musical form that's still unexplored, even now, twenty-five years since this single was released. I'd go so far as to say that there's no way to represent on paper, with current notation, the lyrics, melody, rhythm, or arrangement of this song and come remotely close to what the listener actually hears and experiences. And of course it also flies in the face of conventional wisdom that anything so wildly experimental and avant-garde could be so popular, so dumb and friendly and instantly accessible. Unselfconsciousness is the key. Brian is so keen to please us, and to get into music certain feelings that he knows we feel, too, that he invents a whole new musical language without necessarily realizing it, innocently finding the shortest distance from here to here, it's simple, bass guitar sounds like this, handclaps here, sing this in this pitch, this in this other pitch and right here, lyrics vanish into falsetto here, chorus comes out of the clear blue sky with an attack like *this,* I'll keep the tempo, ready now? Let's go—

And you look back and you've just crossed hyperspace. Hey, that's cool. Listen, bring this master tape to Capitol and tell 'em it's the next single. And could you get us some milkshakes?

*First release:* Capitol 5174, May 1964

# 25 Martha and the Vandellas

## *Dancing in the Street*

Bring the millenium. Whether your vision of the apocalypse is religious (trumpet blowing, the dead rising from their graves) or political (streets and steps filled with people who won't be denied any longer) or simply ecstatic, this record seems guaranteed to push your buttons, to conjure up your vision in no uncertain terms. Dance records tend to be, and usually intend to be, ordinary, repetitive, safe, but there is nothing ordinary about this one. It unfailingly evokes the exceptional—one of the first true planetary songs, an anthem for all spontaneous gatherings, all sudden outpourings of free human energy. The songwriters and producers probably didn't conceive of it this way, but anyone who hears "Dancing in the Street" immediately recognizes it as a or even the quintessential hymn of revolution, riot, and rapture.

And our natural response is, we want to join the party.

So okay, having acknowledged the song's Significance, I need to find a way to explain something difficult, which is that it is ultimately the *sound* of the record, rather than what it means (to me or anyone else), that determines its greatness. This is confusing, because I could also say that the sound of the record gives it its meaning, which is true, and then it might seem again like "meaning" is the ultimate determinant, or at least an always convenient reference point for discussing why a song is loved.

But I say the sound is the more accurate reference point, because meaning is generated by our response to the sound, and for a record to be truly great, truly alive, it must have the power to generate new meaning every time we listen—not necessarily different, not necessarily the same, but necessarily fresh and of the moment. A great sound, to me, is something alive, that can be returned to again and again as a source of inspiration and nourishment. An explanation of what a song means, on the other hand, is dead, not alive; it becomes stable information; it doesn't change; it suggests a predetermined response.

Great rock and roll records refuse to be limited to attached, remembered, predetermined responses. Part of their greatness is their continuing power to break through such straightjackets and waken us to this new reality in which we're living.

Let me further clarify that to me the lyrics are part of a record's sound, in the sense that words (or the sound of words) generate different images depending on how and when they're heard, and depending on the synergy between the sound of the words (or the images they provoke or the feelings aroused through the stories they tell) and the sound of the music, of the rhythm, of the singer's voice. It all works together, the elements of the performance have a collective impact, and it's a trick of the mind that makes us think after the fact that we can separate out the words and use them to measure what the song's "about."

So: forget what you remember, and listen again to "Dancing in the Street." It sounds magnificent. The horn riff that begins it. Martha Reeves' amazing voice, and the space the record builds around it, some kind of unique landscape, you can almost see it, all shadows and light, darkness and depth. And the incredible crash of the beat—rumor has it producer Ivy Joe Hunter banged tire chains on the floor to get the sound he wanted—it sounds simple but you can't get the same feeling from any other record. The sublime drive and ferocious intensity of James Jamerson's bass-playing. "Calling out around the world . . ."

I'm not saying this song has a great message. I'm saying the power of the performance and the response it provokes in us *are* the message. We hear this sound and know without a doubt that yes, the time is right. Whatever that may mean.

The music comes first. With it, we create our own history.

*First release:* Gordy 7033, July 1964

# 26 The Kinks

## *You Really Got Me*

Possession. As in, *possession.* "You got me so I don't know what I'm doing." It can be a peculiarly satisfying state of mind, even though the probable subtext is "I don't got you." But this classic work of musical art goes beyond boy/girl to deal directly with the state of being that frustrated and impassioned boy/girl stuff produces, a state often arrived at through other passions and frustrations as well, a state of joyous self-directed more or less contained violence, over-excitement, over-the-edgeness, screaming inside, screaming outside if you can get away with it, and loving every moment of it, a state of feeling possessed . . . by life, by love, by aliveness, by irrational fascination. Now imagine capturing the *sound* of this. Folding the whole feeling into two minutes and thirteen seconds, with such attention to detail (I didn't say "careful" attention) that twenty listenings in a row won't exhaust the surprises, the richness, the resonating, throbbing bliss of the experience. Here is truth. Here is the anguished, joyous, claustrophobic, liberating, beat-your-head-against-the-door, ultimately unspeakable essence of adolescence—and not just adolescence, though we're most in touch with it then. Rock and roll at its best is the raving, gleeful self-expression of the terminally inarticulate, and we all recognize ourselves in its mumbled shrieks. "You got me so I can't sleep at night! Oh, no . . ." A complaint and a boast.

Is this music? I'm here to argue that, noisy and "anti-beautiful" as this crude recording may sound to unreceptive ears, it is in fact music as good as it gets, comparable to the outstanding works of classical, jazz, or traditional folk/ethnic music-makers; the musical language is different (arising to fit the environment and meet the needs of the times) but the intent and accomplishment and ultimate impact are closely related. I'll even assert that "You Really Got Me" is a thing of beauty, functioning perhaps at cross-purposes to the commonly held image of beauty precisely because beauty is ultimately stifled and lost when the necessary conditions for its existence become too well defined. So the alienated and disaffected become the visionaries, working in the forbidden zone to rediscover the vitality that has been lost in the insecure and therefore deadening, excessively careful mainstream. Kick out the jams. Mutilate the speakers in your worthless little stage amplifier until your guitar sound begins to accurately convey all the angry dirty fuzziness of what you really feel. Attack the drums, hurt them, fall over into them.

But this is mere prelude. Honesty and vitality count for a lot, but actual beauty is transcendent, illuminating the normally perceived world and making us thrillingly aware that there is something more here, something deeply satisfying and arousing, awakening, a divine presence, something worth taking another breath for even though all of our conscious needs and problems remain unmet and unresolved. I'm saying I feel it when I put on the headphones and play "You Really Got Me" at ear-splitting volume, feel it as much today as when I was sixteen, and not as some kind of nostalgia. It takes courage. You blow out the nostalgia with the first few listenings, just as you can blow out your ideas about what's pretty and what's not and whether or not you speak the language. And then, if the work of art happens to speak to you, happens to be tuned to your soul like Monet for me but Gauguin for some other person, if this is a beauty your heart can respond to, terror! as the universe opens up, your private universe melts down and opens up and you fall through the floor of it. You may feel yourself possessed by forces unnameable, clenching your fists and rocking and screaming with fury, passion, joy. The scary thing is that the music, beautiful as it is, doesn't create this. It only triggers it, sets it free.

You really got me. I am really caught by you. This is truth for me, at this moment. I am filled and bursting with it, intoxicated by it, bleeding from it, can't live without it. Play the song again, please. I am starting to have a sense of my own existence.

*First release:* Pye 7N 15673 (U.K.), July 1964

# 27 Them

## Baby Please Don't Go/ Gloria

Into the heart of the beast. Like "Mona," like "Peggy Sue," here is something so good, so pure, that if no other hint of it but this record existed, there would still be such a thing as rock and roll. Essence. It permeates this 45, leaks through from one side to the other and back again. Van Morrison is the singer of both songs, Jimmy Page the lead guitarist on "Baby Please Don't Go" and maybe "Gloria." Plus some other guys, not famous, but the fact is you can't begin to approach the wild grace of these two performances unless you have a terrific rhythm section, I don't mean adequate, I mean inspired incandescent & incomparable. (The rhythm section, bass, drums, sometimes rhythm guitar, is the fountainhead of rock and roll, underrated and underappreciated because its very invisibility is the key to its power. You don't see it or hear it, not really. But you feel it. And everything else is built on and comes forward from the energy field the rhythm section generates. In the case of these performances, it's an energy field so intense and primal that in a sense Van Morrison's and Jimmy Page's much celebrated careers still shine with a little of its reflected light.)

Into the heart. Van Morrison's voice a fierce beacon in the darkness, the lighthouse at the end of the world. "I'm gonna shout it out now/I'm gonna shout it every day/Yeah yeah yeah yeah yeah yeah . . ." Declaration of existence. Organ riff, drum riff, guitar riff—the song ("Gloria") lasted fifteen or twenty minutes when they played it live, they had to compact it into a 2:37 single and they didn't leave anything out.

Resulting in one of the most perfect rock anthems known to humankind. Wasn't even a hit, except locally in certain cities in the U.S., back when there was still such a thing as a regional breakout. But it's made an indelible impression on every rock 'n' roller who's ever heard it. In England the other side, quintessential electric blues like you always hear live but almost never on record, "Baby Please Don't Go" (by Big Joe Williams, or anyway he made it his own), got into the top 10, Ireland's contribution to the U.K.-centered world music explosion. One of the more kinetic performances ever pressed onto plastic. Heavy metal could just as well begin and end with this record. Everything that can happen between lead guitar and bass and singer and listener is at least implied here, "my baby leaving on that midnight train/and I'm crying," you become the train and you become the piercing train whistle in the jilted lover's ears and most of all you become his paradoxical, uncompromising response: cool electric scream of uninhibited self-awareness.

Words can't describe it. Worlds within worlds exist to be explored here, the strength and mystery of these two performances undiminished as the decades go by, just as the mystery of their subject matter, male/female and the feelings sexual connection generates in each of us, never diminishes. Essence. It's in the guitar sound captured herein (lead and rhythm both), and the sound of the whole band as they interact with each other, and the sound of the singer's voice as he spells out the letters of his baby's name.

Them as a band on these two tracks sings with one voice, not Van Morrison's voice though God knows that should be enough for us, but rather the voice of a collective entity, a gestalt, five or six musicians speaking as one from the mysterious center of their collective being, a place of unimaginable simplicity and power.

In most cultures it is forbidden for ordinary persons to own or handle spirit objects. Too dangerous. The priests intervene for our own protection. They confiscate all evidence of spirit's omnipresence, or cloud our minds so we won't perceive it. But ours is a time of transition, and some things slip through the cracks. . . .

*First release:* Decca F 12018 (U.K.), November 1964

# 28 Sam Cooke

## *A Change Is Gonna Come*

This one makes it on the lyric alone. Sam Cooke's vocal is absolutely exquisite, of course, but the only thing "rock and roll" about this record is its message, the simple power of the title phrase, as sung by a black man (a recently dead black man) in America on the public airwaves in 1965.

And that's enough. Or is it? You know, even as I'm writing this entry I could change my mind, take this one off the list and put something else on, decide that it's great but it's not rock and roll, decide that it's a very very good single but not one of the 100 best. Crumple up this piece of paper and toss it aside.

But I won't. I did have it down as a double-sided entry—"Shake," the bigger hit of the two sides, is also delightful—but I changed my mind, sticking to my criterion not to include both sides of a single unless I would include either side by itself. "Shake" is sweet but can't pass that test. "Change," on the other hand, I try to brush off and it won't go away. It insists on being included. It's a song, a performance, of incomparable dignity:

> It's been a long
> A long time coming, but I know oh-oo-oh
> A change is gonna come
> Oh yes it will.

Voices speak to us out of the air, speak so directly to our inner selves we can't help but listen. It seems silly to say God speaks through popular songs, but where else, if anywhere? (And if nowhere, what lonely creatures we are, indeed.) Anyway, God or not, something speaks to us, and sometimes the very simplicity of what we hear is what gives it such tremendous impact. "A change is gonna come." This is a promise, but not only. It's also a gentle reminder that this is something we know, and that when we trust our knowledge it becomes real for us again, an unending source of nourishment. A whisper.

The single is edited from an album track—on the album track, which is three minutes and fourteen seconds long, the mix is different and the violins and horns are too obtrusive. The single version (2:36) gets the sound just right. It omits one verse, serving to make the song a little less obvious in its civil rights message ("I go to the movie/And I go downtown/Somebody keeps telling me/Don't hang around"—this is cut on the single, just before the bridge). But as sometimes happens, the edit actually strengthens the song, providing more ambiguity and more fire for the challenging middle verse, in which the singer asks his brother for help, and "he winds up knocking me back down on my knees." Whew. Tell it like it is.

But what's astonishing is that word "brother." It's bitter, but it's also visionary. The man on his knees can see so much farther than the pitiless (and pitiful) oppressor. He sees a better world, a changed world, not a world of vengeance but one of brotherhood. He sings to raise his own spirits, and to any among us who might waiver in his or her faith. The song is both uncompromising and, implicitly, ultimately, forgiving. Sung by an egotist who apparently died of his own crazed vanity, it is paradoxically a song that expresses true self-love and humility. To hear this song is to have one's personal struggle acknowledged, and to be reminded that there is a gentle, powerful response to oppressive feelings that will, in fact, assure us of victory.

I take back what I said. It's all in the voice, isn't it? And isn't it wonderful when voice and words, spirit and message, are so perfectly united? A great single, call it rock and roll or whatever you want, is a work of art that can instantly bring its listeners to that place where we experience and remember the deepest truths.

It's all in that title phrase, and the way Sam holds it in his heart and voice.

*First release:* RCA 8486, December 1964

# 29 The Who

## *I Can't Explain*

Just what it says. Is what it means. I know you've been there. A person who feels is probably there every time he or she feels anything that's really new and really matters. But until this single was recorded, what hope did she or he possibly have to experience some release in the situation?

This record doesn't actually eliminate the need to punch one's fist through the wall. But at least it provides some companionship during the process.

The Who in their great recordings (most of them singles) are the phenomenally articulate voice of the emotionally tongue-tied, and as such come as close to the pure nature and native purpose of rock and roll as anyone's gotten. I limit myself to three Who A-sides in this book only because the next jump would be eight or so (how about "Substitute"? "Pictures of Lily"? "Pinball Wizard"? "My Generation"? "Anyway Anyhow Anywhere"?) (not to mention some of the greatest B-sides ever, "In the City" and "Baby Don't You Do It" being my particular favorites). These guys are arguably the all-time masters of the three-minute form (if I were to have the argument with myself, you've already sussed that my other candidates would be the Beatles, the Stones, and the Beach Boys; I seem to have a thing for bunches of white, English-speaking males born in the early 1940's) (or more specifically the wheels of plastic they once extruded).

"Three minutes" is an approximation; "I Can't Explain" weighs in at a mere 2:05. "Like A Rolling Stone," coming up later this year, explodes the form by lasting six minutes, but it nonetheless respects and exists in relation to *the form* (honoring it in the breach). It's a great form, terse and to the point, utterly dependent on its ability to catch and hold our attention. Melody, rhythm, language, and performance all in one package, and roughly equal in value (for greatness you must ring all the bells); everything riding on this one song, one statement, one recording. The single. Sole. Soul. I almost *can* explain, that's my problem; my greatest memory of this song is an acid trip in a New York apartment in 1967, me keeping the chaos at bay by figuring it all out very verbally as always, and my lady friend cutting me off, with a playful, wicked grin, saying, "You can't explain." Making me hold my tongue. She had my number, me appreciating it, unspoken excited explanations bursting in my brain and I'd see her smiling and hear this song in my head, superimposed over everything, great tantalizing rhythmic reminder: "I said, 'can't explain.' "

Okay, boss. But— A distinctive aspect of the Who's creative process, right from the beginning, was that the guitar player wrote the songs, working them out on a tape recorder at home and then bringing them down to the studio, like little scripts, a part for each of the four to play, they'd get the drift of it and then run through it like four inspired lunatics, blowing everything but the script apart at every moment, and thereby creating transcendent gems, simple, humorous (musically and lyrically), muscular, subtle, fiercely contained, gloriously violent. "Dizzy in the head and I feel bad/Things you say have got me real mad/I'm getting funny dreams again and again/I know what it means but—"

That perfect last guitar solo (appropriately borrowed from "Louie Louie"; where else?) and the way it segues into the semi-audible (borrowed from the Beach Boys) "ooh ooh"s . . . There's a sweet ringing quality to the guitar and wondrous snap to the drums that isn't quite the same on lp or even CD, you have to hear the Who on seven-inch vinyl to really appreciate them fully. No bull. Worth going to an antique store and buying a phonograph just for the experience. Try it, you'll thank me someday.

*First release:* Brunswick 05926 (U.K.), January 1965

# 30 The Rolling Stones

## *The Last Time*

Is it just loyalty? Is there any way to know? If this hadn't been the record that turned my life around in spring '65, if I were hearing it now more or less for the first time, would I still think it a masterpiece? Yes, I answer, yes of course I would—but I am not an unbiased observer. Are there any such? And if so, do we care a fig for their opinions? Probably not. Probably not. If the Rolling Stones had looked and acted like Herman's Hermits when they weren't performing, would I have fallen in love with them anyway? Probably not—but it's a meaningless question, isn't it? They were who they were. We loved them for who they were, and mostly for the music they made, which was an extension of who they were. It didn't last, but it wasn't an illusion. And, in fact, it lasted for a long, long time.

Never mind. This is not an essay about the Rolling Stones, or about me. It's about this one record. I've told you once and I've told you twice. This could be the last time. Oh no.

Oh yes.

Dave Hassinger is the name of the engineer who got Keith's guitar (and Brian's, too) to sound like that. He was working at the RCA recording studio in Hollywood, California. God bless him. I am a poor man, but I have my riches, and one of them is the sound these guitars make when I listen to this single (no CD, no album or cassette track, not the same I tell you) with the treble up. It's a sound that calls forth the life in me. Always has and still does. Music everlasting.

The engineer did his job.

So let us consider the riff. It's pretty amazing, isn't it? Keith plays the same figure over and over throughout every verse of the song (it's somewhat different—and buried—on the chorus), and through the instrumental breaks, too, repeating it, like a drone, a mantra, one of those Eastern devices that doesn't make a lot of sense to a western set of values . . .

until you hear it, until it grabs you and pulls you under and makes you graphically aware of its power. Oh yes, repetition. Repetition. Now I get it. Like the blood pulsing through my veins and arteries. Not entirely alien after all.

Relentless, however. I can hear it now. I can't describe it in words, only name it: that riff from "Last Time." Over and over, against Jagger's raspy, melodic singing, against the richness and sureness of the rhythm section, against Brian's occasional (breathtaking) grace notes—his lead line just at the end of the first long instrumental break is so astonishing, the way it drops off into the air, you can feel the room, a tangible presence, Hassinger's genius (and Brian's, too, of course). Over and over. Pulling at the threads of context, redefining reality by sheer steadiness, doggedness, force majeure.

The subject addressed so well is indecision, trying to declare an end to something and seeing it go on and on and on anyway, talking tough but still caught on the hook. The endless fade is radical, brilliant, God it sounded so good on a transistor radio (especially the transition into it, drop-out and scream), finally the deejay would start talking over it at the end but only an imbecile would interrupt or fade it early. We're talking holy noise here, sacred writ.

And then "Play With Fire" on the other side, not a "100 Best" song by itself perhaps but close, and absolutely the perfect thing to listen to after playing "The Last Time" four times in a row, a treasure, reason enough to love the Stones right here on side A and side B. Voice of the moment. Unmistakable. If the moment hadn't existed, we would have had to create it, out of the hunger we felt for this music just before it came along.

How the riff transforms the simple-minded drive of the song into something transcendent, point counterpoint, night blossoms shooting color through the darkness. A jumping-off place for many musics to come, from heavy metal to punk to psychedelia. An untoppable opener. Play it again. This could be the last time. Probably not, though. Probably not.

*First release:* Decca F 12104 (U.K.), February 1965

# 31 Bob Dylan

## *Subterranean Homesick Blues*

Having put seven-inch vinyl on a pedestal elsewhere, I want to acknowledge that the compact disc mix of this one cannot be improved upon. Sensational.

When this record came out I was critical of Dylan for the monotonous rhythm, his narrow idea of how to make rock and roll. I was so utterly wrong—it's sobering sometimes to look back on one's past pronouncements. This is a great performance, and every year it sounds better to me. Dylan made rock and roll in exactly the best possible way: no preconceptions whatsoever. "Subterranean Homesick Blues" is, quite simply, contemporary poetry (rapping, verse-making) as good as it gets, rock and roll singing as good as it gets (one of the great vocalists of the century), and small-combo live performing as good as it gets. It's also not like any other Dylan song, though it does have its precursors—Chuck Berry's "Too Much Monkey Business"—and of course its progeny (R.E.M.'s "It's the End of the World as We Know It" springs to mind).

What makes art? What you have to say, the way you say it, how well you say it (impact on audience), and who you are as you say it. You can have "something to say" when you're writing the words of a song, something to say (often a feeling) when you're composing the music, and something to say as you're performing (singing, playing an instrument). Doesn't have to be the same "something"; it just has to all be moving in the same direction.

Words, music, performance (singing), and performance (playing) are different forms of expression that combine to make a recorded song. The power of Bob Dylan's recordings is so great that a listener may be moved to self-defense instead of or in addition to appreciation. One (unconscious) defense is to separate the elements of the experience, as when people say "he's a great writer, but I can't stand his voice." That's a paradoxical statement but not an illegitimate one. Love and hate can be very close at times; indeed, we hate love for making us so vulnerable. Embrace the message, attack the messenger. A good messenger makes use of, encourages, this process. If they reject messenger and message, he's failed. If they receive message and satisfy themselves with the symbolic act of rejecting the deliverer, he's done his job.

It's a struggle for survival. We have to resist the killer of who we've been, even as we welcome the liberator of who we're becoming. The artist unconsciously acknowledges this by following his instinct, which is to wear a mask. The mask says, "This isn't real." We relax, suspend our defenses; as a result, something real can happen. This is the essence of performing, of the artistic process: a conspiracy between creator and recipient, in which we pretend something isn't real so that we can be free to express and receive it fully.

Dylan's great prop or mask is his assumed accent, that obviously false yet extraordinarily durable Okie twang, telling you and himself, "I am an actor, this is an assumed identity, let's pretend this isn't really me and I'm not really speaking straight at you." It allows him (and us) the rich humor that permeates every line of the song, every phrase of the (deadpan) vocal performance ("I'm on the pavement, thinking about the government"). It allows the frightening honesty and directness of this political statement aimed right at the "kids" Dylan imagines listen to the radio (as *he* did as a still-forming adolescent): "Get born, keep warm/Short pants, romance, learn to dance/Get dressed, get blessed, try to be a success/Please her, please him, buy gifts, don't steal, don't lift/Twenty years of schoolin' and they put you on the day shift." The immediacy of the language is also its durability; it will be appreciated forever, like Shakespeare. If we had recordings of Shakespeare performing we might find his voice as grating, and ultimately as irresistible, as Dylan's.

"Look out, kid—" It's a warning. A portrait. A declaration of camaraderie. A stand-up comedy routine. A virtuoso display. A scream. An expression of self. A rock and roll single. A work of art.

*First release:* Columbia 43242, March 1965

# 32 The Beatles

## *Ticket to Ride*

So often it is the color of the painting that attracts us. It seems impossible that every painting should be a different color (how many colors can there be in the universe?), but there can be little question that, in fact, every great painting has a distinguishable tint and pigmentation all its own. "Ticket to Ride" doesn't sound like any other record ever made. Its words, its structure, even its tune are fairly ordinary, and yet there is something about the song, the recording, that is strikingly unusual and immensely appealing. If it were a painting it would be its color—warm, enticing, deep, vibrant—and its texture. It's like I want to live (or at least go for long visits) in the world of this song's sound.

"Ticket to Ride" was written by John Lennon, and he sings the lead vocal; but it would be a mistake to give him all the credit for the masterpiece that results. First of all the most distinctive element in the recording is the lead guitar riff that opens it and threads through it, which is played (and was presumably created) not by John or by George (as I'd always assumed, making me think he was perhaps the most soulful of the Beatles) but by Paul McCartney. Paul also plays bass and is credited in the book *The Beatles Recording Sessions* with having suggested the drum pattern Ringo plays here, another primary element in the freshness and specialness of the song's sound. The third identifiable contributing factor in "Ticket to Ride" 's brilliant freshness is the sound of the vocals. The hook in the song (that element that creates in the casual listener a hunger to hear the song again, vital to selling records and building radio station audiences) is—along with the bursts of crystalline lead guitar at the start of the song and twice in the middle—the way they sing "tod*ay*, yeah" and "aw*ay*" and "d*ow*n, yeah" and "ar*ou*nd" at the end of the verse lines. I say "they" because it's a harmonic effect, probably achieved in part by a doubling or more than doubling of John's voice, but I also hear a flavoring

—just enough to add color, add spice—of Paul and George's voices throughout this "solo" vocal. In any case, whoever's singing, we know enough of the Beatles' recording techniques to know that the creation of the vocal sound was a collaborative process, in which at least Paul and John, and possibly all four plus producer and perhaps engineer, would toss ideas back and forth, experimenting intensely, searching for something, creating together. Another hook (the Beatles never liked to rely on just one hook; that might be good enough for a top 10 single but not a #1) is the gliding vocal that climaxes the chorus, "ri-*hi*-hide." Whose idea? It could have been the singer's, but didn't have to be; and if it was his, he likely wouldn't have come up with it away from the interactive maelstrom of collective creation, the Paul-and-John environment, which, in turn, was always a Paul-and-John-in-relation-to-Paul-John-George-Ringo-George Martin environment, the individual within the partnership within the group. The bottom line is that "Ticket to Ride" is a spontaneous (worked over, but in a brief, intense, spontaneous burst, specifically three and a half hours on the afternoon of February 15, 1965, in Abbey Road studio) masterpiece that could not and would not have been created by John Lennon on his own. It is an expression of the genius of a gestalt: the Beatles. The whole that is greater than the sum of its parts.

If John were still alive people would still be trying to put the gestalt back together, but only because we fail to understand that a gestalt is not simply a group of persons (not that that's simple!) but a group of persons *in and at a particular moment.* The moment comes out of nowhere, lasts as long as it lasts (typically, twenty minutes; in the case of the Beatles, eight years), and then vanishes again, and when it's gone the people look at each other and don't know what they're doing here.

"I think I'm gonna be sad . . ." The girl, the spirit, was here and now she's gone. She's got a ticket to ride, biggest ticket ever written in modern pop culture history, but it doesn't matter, when it's over it's over. And we don't have to be sad. We can thank God instead that we were chosen to be visited by the Mystery.

*First release:* Parlophone R 5265 (U.K.), April 1965

# 33 The Byrds

## *Mr. Tambourine Man*

Circular. All records go 'round, but this one is definitely rounder than most. Mysterious. Here it comes, there it goes, what was that?, here it comes again. Seems like you're just getting into it when it's over, but it doesn't leave you feeling it's too short, just that you missed something, something very special actually, got to listen again and pay more attention this time. And the next time you space right out again. Waking up as you hear that gorgeous electric bass/twelve-string guitar lick that opens and closes the circle, like a finger-snap, into and out of hypnosis, where am I? What just happened? Let's try that again—

What's interesting about the story of this record is the number of people who seem to deserve some credit for it turning out the way it did (weird, perfect, epochal). Producer Terry Melcher was responsible for the Beach Boys ("Don't Worry Baby") influence on the harmonies, tempo, and overall sound. He also chose the session musicians who recorded the instrumental tracks, all masters of the art who outdo themselves on this one: Hal Blaine on drums, Larry Knechtal on bass, Leon Russell on guitar (Roger McGuinn of the Byrds did play the twelve-string on the recording). Jim Dickson, the Byrds' manager, is the one who played them the early dub of "Mr. Tambourine Man," and insisted, over their protests, that they record a demo of it. The Byrds themselves (McGuinn, Gene Clarke, David Crosby, Chris Hillman, Mike Clarke) deserve credit for the arrangement, the concept, which was then embellished and improved by producer and studio musicians. And of course McGuinn (lead) and G. Clarke and Crosby (harmonies) are responsible for the dreamy, impersonal (sounds like a voiceover from somewhere deep in our collective unconscious), magnificent vocals. And then there's Bob Dylan, whose words and melody, however transformed (the Byrds' version includes only one of the song's four verses), are still the primary attraction here. Amazing, isn't it, when you want to single out one person (Roger McGuinn, John Lennon) and identify his genius as the explanation for the miracle, how much more subtle and complex the actual creative process turns out to be! The more one learns about how things really happen, I say, the more reason one finds to believe (in one's heart if not in one's mind) in a higher power that choreographs all our little dances for its own amusement and aesthetic satisfaction.

Ya did good this time, zeitgeist, old friend.

This was arguably a breakthrough moment in the development of rock and roll as an overtly inclusive, expansive, cutting-edge art form. The Beatles and the Beach Boys (not to overlook Buddy Holly and Chuck Berry before them) had already been successfully incorporating any and all musical influences that struck their fancy into the pop music/rock and roll hit singles they created; but the Byrds' "Mr. Tambourine Man" (and its success, inevitable once the first L.A. radio stations jumped on the record—Billy James probably deserves the credit for that part of it) had the effect of announcing explicitly that this is what rock music is and can be: a forum for presenting avant-garde language (musical and poetic) to an intelligent, receptive mass audience, not watered down (not necessarily watered down) but transformed, focused, intensified. In the short run it may have spawned a silly trend ("folk rock") and a bunch of boring, soundalike records; but in the long run, it opened the door for the next wave—Buffalo Springfield, Jefferson Airplane, the Doors, the Grateful Dead, Jimi Hendrix, the overtly eclectic Beatles ("Yesterday," *Sgt. Pepper*)—and, more immediately, for Dylan himself, weeks after the Byrds' record broke, to go and record his radical new music (not at all like "Tambourine Man" in sound or lyric content) directly for this new audience whose existence the Byrds asserted by singing to them over every radio in the land.

Exciting times. But never mind. Throw all that away and this is still a great record. Evokes drug use, sure. Evokes *every* altered state. Hypnotic words, hypnotic voices, hypnotic guitars, hypnotic melody. "Cast your dancing spell my way . . ." Pied piper music. Good thing it isn't just one person's creation. He'd have a lot to answer for.

*First release:* Columbia 43271, April 1965

# 34 The Rolling Stones

## (I Can't Get No) Satisfaction

You could think of it as some sort of grim pursuer, that riff, ominous, relentless, following the singer, the protagonist, the persona who speaks and with whom we identify. And—it suddenly occurs to me, after twenty-four years of chewing on the matter—the riff consists not of the eight repeated fuzz-tone guitar notes alone, but of guitar *and* drums, together, that's the riff, the combination of the two, running parallel throughout the song, not something you can write music notation for, it has to be experienced, heard, felt. One of the more physical, tactile recordings ever made by white musicians. Again a nod to Hassinger please, and to Keith who wrote and performs the guitar part of the riff and came up with the title phrase, and to Mick who sings, acts, and shakes his voice in our face here like no one before or since, but most of all let us give credit where credit is due: Charlie Watts. His record. Charlie manages to be both the pursuer and the pursued, the sound of both, the tangible presence of both, my restlessness and that which won't give me rest, Charlie's drumming creates it, expresses it, releases it, like nothing before or since, which is why late one night I heard a deejay in Troy, New York, play this record three times in a row and declare it our new national anthem. International anthem. Transtemporal. *This* is what it means to be a teenage male, and not only. It is also present in us all, any sex, any age, buried or right on top, all the time. Can't get no. An exaggeration, perhaps, but a truthful exaggeration. This is what it feels like. And this is what to do about it. Listen to Charlie. Again and again and again.

What is it that's after us? Certainly among other things it is the times themselves, and of course we're also the engine driving them forward as fast as they'll go, faster than we can bear, push, pull, we are the oppressed and we are the oppressor.

Modern age. Factory. Jet plane. Power. Noise. "I would tear this building down." Rock and roll speaks to and of that part of us that is excited about change and angry about change and hungry to make this changing, angry, exciting world its own. Our own. We express in order to get out from under and seize the reins. Turn up the volume. Make the music louder, shake my bones till they rattle, shake the walls of the empire. Scream louder than the buzzing in our ears. Reclaim the space. Rock and roll's a prime tool for the job, we know it when we hear it, shock of recognition. I hear it coming, the beast of the age, and my heroic response is to pretend to be the beast myself, but wiser, younger, more beautiful, more outrageous. Scare it off, take its place. Revolution. Is this mere folly? Folly yes, but maybe not mere. The walls of the city do shake, and my bones also. This crashing drumbeat must be an authentic statement.

Yes, I feel it, I know that it is. It has heart. It is personal, and collective, at once. It speaks for our moment.

What the enemy—which is time, cowardice, laziness, fear, ambition, Logos-worship—will try to do is turn it into a nostalgic object. A symbol of some lost or remembered time. Bullshit. This record moves the heart, or it is nothing. Moves the present-day heart, touches me, shakes me, redirects my life. Is dangerous. Is not a symbol of anything. Is not for sale. Does not belong to the musicians or the record company. Does not belong to the person writing about it. Belongs only to the listener at the moment of contact. Guitar/drums riff and vocal tour-de-force hammering and dancing, through body and brain. Endlessly, eternally satisfying. A contradiction. I am fulfilled. I want more. "I just can't be satisfied," Muddy Waters said that. "Just can't keep from trying." Start the machine. Bum bum, ba ba ba, ba ba, ba; bum bum, ba ba ba . . . (bam bam bam bam bam bam bam bam)—

*First release:* London 9766, June 1965

# 35 Wilson Pickett

## *In the Midnight Hour*

It gets into the blood. That horn riff, the powerful, unusual rhythm ("fractionally delayed backbeat"), those fat, beautiful bass notes, Pickett's astonishing voice (as a sound, an instrument, a texture), and after a while you're dancing not only to the record on the phonograph but to an internal recording pounding and pulsing through your veins, you can play the instrumental track at will in your mind and then, when you drop it from consciousness, it's still there in your body, vestigial, permanent, like the salty ocean water we once lived in, BUM ba ba bum, ba ba bum ba ba bum ba ba bum, melodic rhythmic living fragment of human spirit (made in Memphis), lodged in the circulatory system from where it eternally nourishes the involuntary nervous system, "play it for me one time now," all right! And on top of all this, a great vocal performance, the sort of spirit that gets flowing at the peak moments of a four-hour show at the Apollo Theater, too intimate to be captured on vinyl but there's always an exception. Jerry Wexler, who brought Pickett from New York to record with the Stax house musicians at their studio in Memphis, told an interviewer, "It was different down there, it veered away from formal, written arrangements and back to head arrangements. By that I mean it put the creative burden back on the rhythm section, to a symbiosis between the producer and the rhythm section. You don't know why you're doing it—maybe some of it comes from subconscious memory. But it's southern, very southern. Which is to say extremely ad-lib." That's the creation of the sound. And the job of that sound is to set the singer and audience free (of all earthly distractions and shackles), so they can have an experience of what Prince calls "Uptown." Totally Uptown. A level of musical communication so intimate, so visceral, and so sophisticated that if you haven't been there you can't even imagine it. A shared moment. The midnight hour.

The midnight hour. Stax guitarist/songwriter Steve Cropper

noticed Pickett using the phrase as part of his song-ending rap on some live recordings ("wait for the midnight hour, baby"), and suggested building a song around it. They did so, and thereby changed (added to) our language, our ability to talk about the human experience. "I've been planning for years to write a book about the midnight hour, which to me is a certain place beyond or outside of time that I have visited again and again, in a special moment with a friend, on a sexual adventure, at a party particularly a party that lasts for days, like a convention or other gathering, sometimes listening to music or all alone and for no reason at all, boom, I'm in that timeless place, and I love it. All of your past and future are with you in the midnight hour." That's from a book of mine called *Waking Up Together;* the point is, I consider this record—its title, its mood, and its sound and lyrics—to be a left-handed description of a real place I've been to many times, often in the specifically romantic and sexual context that this record refers to, but not only. The only other name I know for this mood or condition (most of all it's a particular time or place that exists outside the normal rules of time and space) is timelessness. Dylan's recording of "Mr. Tambourine Man" speaks of it obliquely: "Play a song for me/I'm not sleepy and there is no place I'm going to/ . . . In the jingle-jangle morning I'll come following you." This is a special, blissful moment separated from the "real world" by the practical privacy of deep night. Staying up after the day-timers have konked out; they've gone to unconscious dreamland leaving us free to play in waking dreamland. "I'm gonna do all the things I told ya, in the midnight hour."

This record doesn't just introduce or name this vital environment. It also embodies it; captures the sound and feeling of it; affirms and indeed proves its existence. Makes it available and accessible (it already is, always is; but sometimes we have to be able to see or touch—or hear—the open door in order to walk through it). What more could a record, or any human artifact, possibly deliver? Hats off to Pickett, Cropper, Jackson, Dunn, Stewart, Wexler, and the horns, for their remarkable creation. "I'm gonna hold you in my arms in the midnight hour."

*First release:* Atlantic 2289, June 1965

# 36 Bob Dylan

## *Like A Rolling Stone*

I have heard so many different things in this song at different times. It is a deep pool of shimmering water, that gives off one reflection from its surface, and others when one's eye is drawn into the depths. And naturally the content of the reflection changes depending on who is looking, and when. "How does it feel?" The question is always relevant, and the answers are never the same. Most of all what we feel is the impact of that voice, so individual and intimate, a visit from a whole different order of reality, opening new realms, probably very much like what Robert Zimmerman felt when Little Richard's voice first spoke to him across the night airwaves.

*"Ah,* you never turned around to see the frowns on the jugglers and the clowns when they all did— tricks for you." Ostensibly he's speaking to a woman (fallen woman, was dressed fine, now scrounging, the singer plays a jilted lover imagining sweet revenge), but perhaps we can also recognize here (from our own experience) the voice of conscience, self-criticism, self-awareness. Notice the grace and power of the internal rhyming: "around, frowns, clowns." This pattern is used throughout the song, starting with "time, fine, dime, prime" in the opening sentence. Dylan's language—images, choice of words, the pertinence of his observations—is so entrancing we don't always notice his skillful structural inventions, even as they work their magic on us. The first two lines of each stanza of "Like A Rolling Stone" use internal rhymes to create a rhythm, a kineticism, a feeling of building up to something; they also rhyme or almost rhyme with each other, in zany three-syllable mini-climaxes ("juiced in it," "used to it"). The four middle lines rhyme with each other, each phrase building on the one before; and the last line rhymes with the first line of the chorus, setting up a huge release on the word "feel." Tension is then built up again through another sequence of four rhyming lines ("own," "home," "unknown," "stone"). Thus the

rhyme structure mirrors and interacts with the steadily rising tension and the series of mini-releases built into the music of the song.

The craft involved here is awe-inspiring, and is obviously a combination of conscious intent and unplanned, spur-of-the-moment invention. Dylan the performer takes things a step further, dropping and adding lyrics as he sings, lengthening and shortening lines, changing meter, melody, rhythm, timing, making the musicians crazy and using their confusion to spur their creativity. Vocal mannerisms (the four "ah"s, one before each of the last three verses and another amazing one before the final "How does it feel?") become vast embodiments of spirit conjured up by and contributing to the passion of the performance. Everything works together, not by design but by sheer willpower, force of personality.

Listen to Dylan's voice as he sings ". . . tricks for you." There is a presence, a personality, a tone of voice, sarcasm, humor, intensity, so much aliveness every second, one doesn't have to focus in to feel the impact, even chopped in half for quicker airplay this performance captivated a generation, as it inevitably would any generation that (and this is not inevitable) gave it space to be heard and accepted it as something of their own, mysterious all-encompassing anthem of who we are and how it feels to be this way.

Who are we? According to this song, nobody: alone, no home, unknown, invisible, got nothing to lose, no secrets, living on the street. And, funny thing, as we sing along with the stirring chorus, it actually sounds like we're *proud* of our condition. How does it feel? By the time the last chorus is chugging along it feels great, and if we stop to reflect we might wonder how we went from such twisted bitterness to such unrepressed joy.

Dylan wrote this song as a prose poem, an attempt to purge himself of fury and vengefulness, frustration with his "career," frustration with himself. It was never meant to be a song, but somewhere along the way it started to have a tune, started to sing to him. So he listened. And learned a new way of singing. And taught it to the rest of us.

*First release:* Columbia 43346, July 1965

# 37 The Beatles

## *Day Tripper*

So if there were no war between men and women, what would become of rock and roll?—answer me that. Love is anger, hunger, desire, frustration, and regret, with a lot of delight and loneliness thrown in, and should peace be declared and all the problems resolved, wouldn't be much left to sing about, would there? But not to worry.

John Lennon was a cad and a curmudgeon, but what matters is, he wasn't afraid to open his mouth and shout his feelings. "She was a day tripper, Sunday driver yeah; it took me so-ooooh long to find out . . . and I found out." And what? Well, you stop panting after her, right? But that leaves you with all kinds of uncomfortable feelings, and there's nothing you can do with them, except maybe scream, loud, and if that feels a little better, then bring in the boys and the electric guitars and drums and let's really get into it.

Actually, according to what passes for history (an interview on the run six months later), the song was written under pressure because "we needed a single." A single. What's a single? A song, a recording, with a good chance of being a hit if it's played over and over again on teen radio. Something that jumps out of the box at you. Not just a wonderful song (like "In My Life") or a memorable song (like "Norwegian Wood") or an immensely clever song (like "I'm Looking Through You" or "I've Just Seen A Face") (all examples from *Rubber Soul,* written and recorded and released more or less simultaneously with the two-sided single "Day Tripper"/"We Can Work It Out"), but a song with some particular quality, a hook, a dignity, an unmistakable and overwhelming sense of identity, allowing it to be sent out there on its own to stand before the world and win people's attention, time, money, love. "Got to come up with a single." Something that'll sell. Where do you turn? A lot of different places, and the Beatles were particularly adept at not repeating themselves, at maintaining their supremacy by constantly coming up with surprises. You turn, if you're unselfconscious artists at the height of your powers, to whatever moves across your consciousness, like, for example, sexual resentment. And a phrase, a hook, an idea, a word. "Day tripper." Maybe from a bus you saw this morning. Maybe it's well-established British slang, I wouldn't know, but it certainly was new to my ears, and so perfect. "Trip" a good word to play with in 1965 anyway. You're a tourist! A tease? Yes, but that's not the focus here, don't dignify her with the power, the intentionality that implies. A Sunday driver, that's all. "I found out!" Dig into that guitar riff. Scream those two-part harmonies now, and turn up the maracas in the mix till the walls shatter. You want a bloody single, do you? Here's your bloody fucking single, you $%*#!s.

Magic. That sound (I bought a UK single and almost scratched the song off my list, for some reason it's the American mix that makes it on this one, like night and day) is so amazing, that riff so deep and clean and forceful and visible, bold fat clanging strokes, fierce and precise, and the voices totally fresh, passionate, full of humor and released frustration and bright revenge. How do you create something like this? Quickly. With intensity. Unselfconsciously. Joyously. And (mask of cynicism can't quite hide your unmistakable commitment) from the heart.

*First release:* Capitol 5555, December 1965

# 38 The Miracles

## *Going to A Go-Go*

In 1967, I suggested to Ray Manzarek that the Doors should record a cover of "Going to A Go-Go." He said something about the importance of a modern rock band writing their own songs, which I thought naive, but anyway it seemed clear he didn't hear the song the way I did. In hindsight I think I was wrong—I heard the song as one of the darkest and most urgent recordings ever to come out of Motown, an evocation of the party mood at the heart of an inner city riot and a (presumably unconscious, unintended) invitation to join in . . . but even if the Doors had managed to recapture in their own version all the delicious ominousness of the three-note riff and the weird transcendent power of Smokey's warbled exhortations ("Yeah! people, come on . . ." "na na na na yeah"), they would have been done in by the lyrics. Jim Morrison's persona just wasn't flexible enough for him to sing "A go-go can't be far-a . . . don't be shocked if you see your favorite star-a" without sounding ridiculous. Maybe the Velvet Underground could have pulled it off.

Musicians lead by following. That's the only plausible explanation I have for how Smokey (and his three co-writers, Tarplin, Moore, and Rogers, same team that put together "Ain't That Peculiar" for Marvin Gaye, another classic) ended up making such a great record out of what was undoubtedly a routine, sleepwalking assignment to come up with an uptempo song based on the latest dance craze (like "Come On, Do the Jerk," another favorite of mine). This is what jazz is all about, isn't it?—the idea that if you go out there and start playing together as a combo you'll hear something living, something unexpected, and by following it together you move away from the merely mental (your plans and preconceptions) and (on a good night) into the true spirituality of music. You jam, as it were, get into a groove, with the living presence of the moment.

That presence seems to come out of the air, but it's actually an extension of the ever-changing awareness—feelings, experiences, life—of the people in the room (other living beings project it, too; take your clarinet out in the woods sometime, and get into a groove with the trees and the insects). The words Smokey wrote for this song are stupid, but the subject matter, though familiar, is very real: the coming together of the community, on its own terms, free of the nine-to-five world of the Man, time to get down, to dance together, to come alive. The riff says night, freedom, danger, action. The ringing sound of the riff (I can't identify the instrument—electric piano? marimba?) is inspiring, electrifying, especially as set against the dark, excited complexity of the bass-playing. The teeming intensity of jungle life—we're talking ecosystem here, not just human culture—is instantly tangible in that hubbub of bass notes, along with a keening individuality. If you want some insight into what soul is, dig what the bass player's getting into here, and then let yourself hear Smokey the singer, same guy who wrote these lyrics on dull automatic pilot (but it doesn't matter, it's just a place to jump off from), responding to what he's hearing in the incredible smoldering tracks the band's laid down. Oo oo ee ee! A one more time, yeah. Now it's all right . . .

Going to a go-go. Superficial level: something's happening, let's make a song about it. Deep level: *some*thing's *happening,* I think we just made a song about it. Whew. All right.

*First release:* Tamla 54127, December 1965

# 39 Shades of Blue

## *Oh How Happy*

Instant relief from depression: slip this single on the phonograph. Works every time. And that's not easy! The cynic inside each of us is strong and versatile, ready with a thousand different reasons to doubt, deny, dismiss. Yet this little performance can disarm him, make him grin, let him (her) relax, and not just for the duration of the tune. A lasting remedy. I guarantee it. Money back if not satisfied.

It's wonderful, when you think about it, what a song, a recording, can do. This is what we love in music, that it is such a source of nourishment to us, a friend, companion, mother, lover. No exaggeration! A source of something we need, many things we need: reassurance, distraction, stimulus, release, courage, acceptance, entertainment. Refreshment. Makes us feel good.

This record's been special to me for a long time, maybe partly because it's not so well known, I admit there are records I've left out of this book only because their popularity or familiarity devalued them for me to some extent, just enough to make them miss the cut. I don't remember how I discovered it, it was after its term on the airwaves I think (hit singles are butterflies with eight-week life spans, or were until oldies became such a big business), probably through a friend or else some accident; all I can remember now is the affirmation in 1969 or so when a friend discovered it in my collection with a wide smile, confiding that she also loved it, used it, believed it to have extraordinary restorative powers.

Released on a tiny Detroit label (Impact), group never heard of before or since, got to #12 on the national charts, its only link with history the song's author (and possibly producer, though he doesn't get the credit), Edwin Starr, who first made the charts in '65 with his own "Agent Double-O-Soul" and later (1970) had a #1 record on Motown called "War." But other than that, the Shades of Blue came and went in pure anonymity, pure as the piano chords that run through this record and the ringing bells at start and finish and the crystalline vocals (solo and chorus) that sparkle from it and carry its message. Came and went but not really; they're still here; in my life and on my phonograph this very afternoon.

Unusual for a rock and roll record (rhythm and blues, actually, but a crossover hit, and therefore a simultaneous citizen of both realms) to address the subject of marital bliss, since teen identification is the sine qua non for a hit single in the rock era. But somehow this one gets away with it, perhaps because "oh how happy you have made me" beautifully expresses the soaring feelings of a young girl after a week's romance, and if she hears the "in our years together we have had stormy weather" part she just changes it to "weeks" or projects it into a great fantasized future. I don't know. I wasn't married or even in a relationship when the song first captured me. Now I can hear the sweet maturity in it, or take it further and apply it to a relationship with the divine (any song of devotion can be extended this way), but the specialness in the record is in the immediacy of its message, the brightness of the performance comes right across regardless of circumstance, it's like you forget the details of your life, and just suddenly remember what it is to be happy.

A hand-clapper. It ends in a round, like "Three Blind Mice" or the Beach Boys' exquisite "God Only Knows." Lifts the spirit, rhythmically, melodically, features gorgeous group crescendoes and moments of touching awkward vulnerability (reaching for a low note), just everything you could possibly want in a record like this, and really there is no other record like this. It's a song of acknowledgment, a song about giving, and it does give; I wonder if the Shades of Blue, whoever they be, have any idea how much they've enriched us, how much we appreciate it, how amazing it is the way gifts just go on giving.

*First release:* Impact 1007, April 1966

# 40 Ike and Tina Turner

## *River Deep, Mountain High*

There's a lot to love on this record, but I can tell you what I like best, at least this week: it's when the break comes in, the start of the bridging verse (it would connect the second and third verses except there is no third verse; instead the bridge leads back to the chorus, and then the song ends), the part where Tina sings "I love you baby like a flower loves the spring," and the syncopated bass line (and maracas) leading into that vocal, and the finger-snapping behind her voice. Something really wonderful happens for me when that transition starts, something I look forward to each time I listen even as I'm enjoying all the other wonderful moments in Tina Turner's vocal performance and Phil Spector's arrangement. George Harrison has called this "a perfect record from beginning to end." I think that's true of most of the entries in this book, but "River Deep, Mountain High" is the sort of record that inspires such comments, not just a tour de force but an *evident* tour de force, self-conscious, proud, and also able to laugh at its own delusions of grandeur. Something imperfect that I like about it is it catches Tina and Phil showing off for each other, which is part of its charm. It's overwhelming and too much and it knows it and thereby manages to be lovable and playful even as it overwhelms. The listener gets to join in the fun, too: "Oh, it's got me, I'm overwhelmed, I'm going under, wee-oooh!"

Transitions. When we examine the amazing constructs known as Beatles records, or Beach Boys records, or Phil Spector records, what we find is two and a half or three minutes jam-packed with extraordinary, inventive, unexpected transitions. Little ones and big ones. The swoop of Tina's voice from vulnerable little girl to passionate man-eater (1.2 seconds) is a transition. The single delayed drumbeat that connects the instrumental lead-in with the first word of the vocal is a brilliantly effective transition, aided and abetted by the absence of instrumentation behind the first five words. The result is that the lead-in stands on its own, as a dramatic statement, as a melodic and rhythmic fragment, and as a delicious hook; the opening of the vocal and introduction of the singer is powerfully dramatized; and the next major transition is set up, the reentry of the band with the word "girl," immediately followed by the entry of the back-up singers going "doot d-doot" behind the vocal. Suddenly we're in a swirling maelstrom of music and rhythm and information, but it's been built up to (in ten seconds), there's a sense of order here, we have an experience of having opened a door, looked inside, and walked through, before being surrounded and swallowed by the noise of the party.

A whole other kind of transition occurs in the middle of the first verse: as Tina moves from "my love has grown" to "and it gets stronger" she changes the sound of her voice, violently, abruptly, invariably sending a shot of adrenaline through the listener's veins. Spector as producer may have been coaxing her to make a shift here, but what she comes up with could never have been scripted ahead of time, nor can it be successfully described after the fact. She twists her voice in the direction of a scream, but not quite, and reaches in with shamanic fingers to make certain very specific and powerful adjustments in the consciousness of the listener. It's done from a place and with a knowledge much older than recorded history, and when she does it to us it not only causes a shift in us but also brings up our awareness that such interactions occur and that we have been a part of them, probably since time began.

The lyrics, corny as they are when considered apart from the performance, successfully make the link-up between lovemaking and memory and the awe we feel in contemplating our trembling existence, depths of the firmament spread below us and the heights of heaven rising above. The singer personalizes this: tells her lover what he stirs up in her. And then allows herself to actually get stirred up, thinking about it.

She acts it out. Catharsis. Instead of a third verse, the bridge takes us into a climactic sequence of speaking in tongues: "Baby. Baby. Baby. Oh, baby! Oh! Oh—"

The births and deaths of galaxies compacted into a few seconds. A good trick if you can do it.

*First release:* Philles 131, April 1966

# 41 The Four Tops

## *Reach Out I'll Be There*

What is an anthem? The usage I've grown up with, where we speak of certain Dylan songs or Stones songs or Chuck Berry songs as teen anthems, rock anthems, implies a stirring song that provides some sense of group identity—"Like A Rolling Stone" expresses something central to who I am and who we are for so many people that it becomes an anthem of the moment or even, to some degree, of the generation. In a more ephemeral sense, songs like "It's My Life" and "We Gotta Get Out of This Place" by the Animals are anthems. The message in the title, which necessarily is also the dominant phrase in the song, jumps out of the radio and we sing along, maybe even shake a fist in the air.

When I look in the dictionary, though, I get "a song of praise or devotion, as to a nation, college, etc." That's not right. "Reach Out I'll Be There" is recognizably anthemic, but it doesn't praise anything—you could say it expresses devotion, but devotion to a person is very different from what the above definition refers to, and anyway that's not what makes this record an anthem. What is it? It's the title, the message expressed in the title phrase, and in particular the way that phrase is used in the song—the way it's built into the song, and the way it's *delivered.*

Lead singer: "Darling—" Backup singers: "reach out . . ." Lead singer: "C'mon girl, reach on out for me." Backup: "reach out . . ." Lead: "Reach out for me." Band: long vamp by rhythm section, broken by an explosive vocalized out-breath from the singer: "Hah!" Backup and lead singer together (this is it, the pay-off, the release, the hook): *"I'll* be there, with a love that will shelter you; *I'll* be there, with a love that will see you through . . ."

It's (I don't have to tell you; you know this) absolutely wonderful. Back to the dictionary, alternate definition of anthem: "Formerly, a religious song sung antiphonally." Hmph. Turn pages, here it is: "Antiphon—a hymn, psalm, etc. chanted or sung in responsive, alternating parts; anything composed for responsive chanting or singing."

Now we're getting somewhere. A song is an anthem based on a certain response it triggers in the listener; a response that specifically has to do with singing along, not because that's the form of the song but because its content, verbal as much as musical, spontaneously inspires such participation. We sing along with the message—we feel it and recognize it as *our* message, something that expresses a core element of our emotional/spiritual existence. Not just a song about love, a song about who I am. I'm the sort of person who is there for you. As Levi Stubbs, lead singer of the Four Tops, says in the record's climactic moment, "Just look over your shoulder!"

Whew. Of course, as in all these great singles, every element contributes. The strings at the beginning, the marching drums, get into the blood immediately, I mean we're standing at attention and waving the flag before we even know what cause we're rallying to. And then Levi's incredible vocal and the music that supports it: "Now if you feel that you can't go on—" That's all he has to say. Already we know he's got the antidote. He's *giving* us the antidote. And then we become him, he's speaking for me, I am the antidote.

"Reach Out I'll Be There" was written and produced by the great team of Brian Holland, Lamont Dozier, and Eddie Holland. I was fascinated to learn how they divided their labors in those days—first Lamont Dozier would come up with a melody and a title, while Brian Holland worked out the structure of the song. Then they'd bring in the band and record the basic track, Lamont supervising the rhythm section, Brian working the engineering board and overseeing keyboards and guitars. Once the track was down, Eddie Holland would come in and write lyrics. Then on to the vocals, with Eddie supervising the lead singer and Lamont in charge of the background vocalists.

Teamwork. It could get mechanical at times, but so much of what they created together was brilliant, and now and then, as on this record, it was pure genius. "I know what you're thinking, you're alone now, no love of your own, but darling—!" It's an anthem. God only knows where such things come from. But you and I know how they feel.

*First release:* Motown 1098, August 1966

# 42 Eddie Floyd

## *Knock on Wood*

Wanna learn to dance? Have I got a record for you. There has never been an easier or more exciting recording to move one's body to than Eddie Floyd's "Knock on Wood," recorded in Memphis's Stax Studios in 1966 with Booker T. and the MGs (Duck Dunn, Al Jackson, Steve Cropper) and one hell of a great horn section. You put this record on and you go out on that floor, with or without a partner, and I guarantee you you'll come to life. You will strut, you will glide, you will shake your hips, you will *emote*—you won't be able to help it. And you won't want to stop. This is glory. This is music that matters.

It matters because dancing matters, because the rhythms of our beingness are just as important as our thoughts (even if the mind don't think so). We are alive while our hearts keep the rhythm going, no longer. Our thoughts in fact are to a large extent just reflections of the rhythms of our experience, our environment, our circulatory systems.

The words of this song are simple and brilliant. I like the way the singer goes from "her love" in the verse to "the way you love me" in the chorus, like an actor on stage first addressing his buddies, then turning and speaking to his leading lady. The twist implicit in the central image is so subtle you might never notice it consciously, yet so powerful you feel its impact in your gut every time you hear it: namely that he's knocking on wood not just for good luck—that he not lose this wonderful woman —but also for protection. "The way you love me is frightening; I think I better knock on wood." Scared to lose her but also scared to be with her, because their loving is so intense.

To say that this intensity is captured in the music that surrounds the words would be an understatement. What we have here, in fact, is a masterpiece of punctuation—rhythm section and horns taking charge of the words, embellishing on them, stopping and starting the flow of spoken language to allow the voices of heart, body, and spirit to be heard. It goes something like this: "I don't want to lose—bonk, bonk—this good thing—bonk, bonka—that I've got (flourish)/'Cause if I do—ba dum dum—I would surely (pause, no change in rhythm), surely lose a lot . . ." Steve Cropper, rhythm guitarist and probably de facto producer, wrote the song with Eddie Floyd, and the two of them have written the sounds of the band into the text of the song—not just the wonderfully dramatic horns and drums but the loping bass that rides along under and between all the other sounds, driving them forward. The end result is simultaneously as loose (in the sense of free, limber, unrestricted) and as tight (in the sense of bright clear colors, sharply defined musical lines, and finely woven interconnection between the various instruments) as any small-combo performance could possibly be. It breathes intensity and sexuality. It's fun. It's charming. It's hot.

Punctuation equals emphasis. Emphasis—where the beat is, and the momentum (or flair) with which you and it move toward and away from each other—is the heart of dance. Emphasis is the content, it's what happens during the two minutes and fifty-five seconds in which singer and band play their song. "It's like thunder . . . lightning . . ." The way it moves me is frightening. And liberating. There's only one appropriate response. "Think I'd better knock, knock, knock on wood . . ."

*First release:* Stax 194, September 1966

# 43 The Beach Boys

## *Good Vibrations*

There has never been anything quite like this. It is a triumph of musical innovation in four or five different areas—song structure, instrumentation, techniques for recording the human voice, techniques for blending and separating (and creating musical transitions between) voices and groups of voices, and most of all new sounds plain and simple, amazing, beautiful, shocking, consciousness-expanding new sounds, like a painter creating new colors, incredible. And at the same time that it burst open vast realms of creative territory, uncompromisingly experimental, "Good Vibrations" was also an instant popular success, the best selling of all the Beach Boys' hit records. It was also the dominant inspiration and goad that drove the Beatles to create some of their most ambitious works. This single, following as it did the Beach Boys' triumphant *Pet Sounds* album, Bob Dylan's *Blonde on Blonde,* and the Beatles' *Revolver,* announced to whomever was interested that contemporary music had moved into a time of competitive creativity comparable to the rush of discovery and invention that marked the first flowerings of Impressionism and Cubism.

Brian Wilson is rock and roll's finest composer ever, and "Good Vibrations" is the most extraordinary of his compositions. (Not my favorite, however; perhaps it's a little *too* perfect.) Basically it expands on a single concept: the line "I'm picking up good vibrations," and the melodic and rhythmic phrase (nine beats) that goes with it. An echoing line is added, same music, different words—"She's giving me excitations." This doubled phrase is then multiplied by four, a repeating chorus. The chorus becomes an implied round as a second set of voices comes in on the second line, laid over the first, singing a harmonic part that takes off from the original phrase—"good, good, good, good vibrations," barbershop quartet stuff, exquisite. The original line is only faintly audible when sung a third time, and the fourth time "good, good, good, good vibrations" takes over completely. A rhythmic shift, specifically a shift of momentum, has also taken place.

This is enclosed within a verse/chorus structure, with a bridging section and then an ending, like "River Deep, Mountain High," the primary outside influence on Brian in the writing of this song (his greatest influence, though, was the progressive development of his own music, as he continued to explore sound and composition by making one record after another—"Good Vibrations" is "Here Today" and "God Only Knows" from *Pet Sounds* multiplied times each other and shuffled together brilliantly, with a triple handful of new ideas thrown in).

So there are four parts: the first begins abruptly with the entry of Carl Wilson's great, soulful, vulnerable lead vocal, "I . . . I love the colorful clothes she wears." The musical track behind him is astonishingly beautiful, haunting, tactile, very simple at first but steadily and subtly building on itself, exploding after the musical transition that leads from the verse to that fabulous, ever-expanding chorus.

First part smacks right into second as the second verse starts —"Close my eyes"—before the last word of the chorus is quite finished. Verse; chorus; and then a sublime musical transition in the middle of the word "excitations" opens us out into part three, a remarkable musical and vocal bridge ("I don't know where but—"), heaven rock at its most transcendent ("ooh my my what a sensation"). Organ and tambourine take us out of the bridge and into the fourth and concluding segment, which begins with the repeated phrase "Gotta keep those lovin' good vibrations happenin' with her" and climaxes in an amazing "aaaahhh!", the official end of the song, after which everything is recessional, the explosive return of the "good good good good vibrations" part of the chorus, then the song's distinctive rhythm figure by itself, then a last burst of heaven rock (four lines of glorious rising harmony—"na na na na na, na-na-na"), with a bit of musical humor as final release and fade-out exit line.

Three minutes and thirty five seconds of genius. And it all reaches our ears as light and breezy and friendly as a warm spring afternoon.

*First release:* Capitol 5676, October 1966

# 44 The Spencer Davis Group

## *Gimme Some Lovin'*

I was visiting a Beach Boys recording session in December 1966 when Carl Wilson walked in with a record he'd just bought, something he'd fallen in love with during the group's recent trip to England. He put it on a turntable, eager to hear it—stopped it after a minute and tried again—then grabbed the record and broke it over his knee in fury. He'd just discovered that the American record company had remixed the song in an attempt to make it more appealing to the American market. The moral is, us fans don't like our music messed with. The record was "Gimme Some Lovin' " by the Spencer Davis Group, and maybe the record company wasn't as stupid as Carl (and I) thought: the Spencer Davis Group had had two previous #1 records in Britain, but the "Americanized" version of "Gimme Some Lovin' " became their first U.S. hit.

Ken Emerson calls "Gimme Some Lovin' " "one of the most excited and exciting vocals ever recorded by a white man." Stevie Winwood was eighteen when he sang and played organ on this straightforward, driving electric blues, written by Winwood with two other band members.

And the question for tonight is, what is "drive" anyway? Because that is what makes this record rock and roll, and also what makes it great: the intensity of its drive. That intensity resonates in shimmering waves from Winwood's voice, in a joyous, unresolved, unresolvable tension, building to a fever pitch through every verse; but the drive itself is most clearly located in the pounding rhythmic figure, bambambambambam, bass drums and rhythm guitar acting as one, that runs through the entire performance, and in the relationship between this riff and the equally driving organ chords that sustain and sustain and sustain, building in pitch along with the vocal and straining every muscle against the rhythmic figure's implicit restraints.

Drive is not velocity but acceleration—the ante must continually be upped. And for it to be communicated effectively (that is, ecstatically) in a rock and roll recording or live performance, there must be a tremendous and very genuine dynamic tension between the musicians, and between the elements of the music that they are creating. It is the fierce pushing against this dynamic tension, combined with the forward momentum of the song itself, that gives the vocal a space in which to express and create so much excitement.

Which is to say, this is not a Stevie Winwood solo record, no matter how hugely his natural talent and ebullient eighteen-year-old presence contribute to it. It is a group performance, and its power comes out of a group dynamic.

The sound, like Hendrix a few months later, is that of musicians accelerating from blues to rock and roll (Hendrix took it a step further; his goal was escape velocity, musical departure for other realities). It is, at this particular moment in the music's life and the musicians' lives, a cry of joy, not a departure from blues but a delighted realization of something one has always heard in it (and always reached for). An expression in new form of what it was that attracted these musicians to the blues in the first place. Something very basic, very sexual, very honest. Very intense.

Drive. It's what gets us up in the morning. Out of our beds and dancing. It's the strength of our youthful spirits, whatever ages we are. It's in the sound. And it's not to be messed with.

*First release:* Fontana TF 762 (U.K.), October 1966

# 45 Buffalo Springfield

# For What It's Worth

I was a fan of Buffalo Springfield from the moment I heard their first single, "Nowadays Clancy Can't Even Sing" ("who's putting sponge in the bells I once rung?"), wafting over the late-night airways. Two months later I was in California for the first time in my life, a young (eighteen) music magazine editor looking up his favorite groups on the pretext of journalism. I heard and met the Springfield at the Whisky A Go-Go on Sunset Strip; they had just recorded a song Stephen Stills, one of the group's three lead singers, had written a few days before, about the Sunset Strip police vs. teens "riots" that had occurred the previous week. They were excited. It was an era, like 1989 in Eastern Europe, when you could get high on the events that were happening around you—and jump in and be part of them whenever you were ready.

"For What It's Worth" is one of the greatest topical songs of its era—but if I may say so, the record is even better than the song. What I'm getting at is something I say a lot when I'm writing about Bob Dylan, which is that when song lyrics stick in our minds and have a great impact on us, the reason is not to be found in the lyrics alone, but in the combination of lyrics and tune and beat and performance and, most of all, *sound,* which is to some degree the sum of the preceding, but it is also something separate, something that has to do (on a record) with the engineer and the room and the board and the unpredictable magic of the moment (we hear less of this magic on modern recordings that encourage too much control and leave too little room for accident).

The *sound* of "For What It's Worth" is absolutely electrifying. (I remember playing it on a jukebox once in a bus station in San Francisco, and hearing and feeling those crystalline lead guitar notes cutting pathways through the dark afternoon air, those deep vibrating bass/snare/foot-pedal notes shaking the building and reawakening my connection to something more solid—it was a brief, very powerful visionary experience in aural and tactile form, unforgettable.) First thing we hear: Neil Young's gentle, penetrating, hauntingly beautiful guitar, followed by an equal, awesome gentleness in the rhythm and vocal performances. The tempo achieved is unique to this record; and certainly it's a rare rock and roll performance that draws its power from its modesty (Chuck Berry's "Memphis" comes to mind). Stephen Stills's vocal is brilliantly underplayed: the calmer his voice is, the more we feel the strength of his conviction and the earnestness of his simple request that we direct our attention here.

Every songwriter of Stills's generation wanted to write a song like Dylan's "Ballad of A Thin Man"; Stills alone succeeded, I think, and in many ways he improves on the original. Like the sound they inspired and emerged out of, these often-quoted lyrics are unforgettable, the voice of their moment and of many more to come: "There's something happening here/What it is ain't exactly clear . . . Stop, hey, what's that sound? Everybody look what's going down."

The message is spiritual as well as political; in true times of change, the two are inseparable. Stills criticizes the police state for the paranoia it creates, its destruction of spirit, and at the same time (as I hear it; it's a song different listeners hear many different things in) cautions his listeners that they themselves have the power to determine whether or not they will let fear rule their lives. Righteousness also gets a firm, if gentle, swat: "Singing songs and carrying signs/Mostly say, 'hooray for our side.' " "Nobody's right if everybody's wrong." The song is a call to awareness and, at least implicitly, resistance, but there is also a plea for brotherhood, a rejection of "us and them" thinking. In short, most of the vital issues are touched on, issues that confuse us (forgetful as we are) to this day. Listen again. Sometimes the voice of the spontaneous, brash teenager is the true voice of wisdom.

*First release:* Atco 6459, January 1967

# 46 Aretha Franklin

## *I Never Loved A Man (The Way I Love You)*

So much can happen in three minutes. This classic single, Aretha's first recording for Atlantic, widely considered her "coming out" as an artist (and, not incidentally, one of the great vocal performances of the century), is so packed with emotional information a thousand computers couldn't hold it, even if they could find some way (other than Aretha's voice) to encode it. The woman was twenty-four years old. Her frustrating six-year relationship with Columbia Records had just ended badly, and now she and her husband/ manager were in a small town in Alabama cutting a song with a bunch of strangers. Later that night he would get into a sequence of drunken fights, first with one of the musicians, later with her, and the next morning the singer and her husband (they split up the following week, got together again a few weeks later) left Muscle Shoals and never returned. (The rest of Aretha's famous "Muscle Shoals" recordings were made in New York, with Muscle Shoals musicians.)

"I Never Loved A Man" is a song about a trapped victim, but that's not the way Aretha sings it. Not that she leaves that part out, but what comes through more than anything is, confoundingly, the singer's strength and self-assurance. "Don't you never never say that we're through" is not a plea (though that side of it is included in her multileveled vocal reading), nor quite a threat (though there's more than a hint of that, too), but rather a confident (despairing but confident) and even affectionate declaration of love.

Politics is often argued as if its issues could be resolved by the intellect alone, which is ridiculous, and all the more so in the case of sexual politics. This song says more about certain aspects of sexual politics than any essay and most novels, and it does so by its uncompromising expression of honest feeling. It's a description of personal reality, a direct sharing of experience, full of twists and mood shifts and contradictions—its power lies in raising questions, not answering them. Its power lies also in the fierce clarity with which it rejects conventional wisdom (without denying the horror of the situation). "I guess I'll never be free" hardly sounds like an affirmation; and yet the way Aretha sings it, you can't be certain it isn't one. She underlines her stand in her frenzied last words before the fade, "Well if you just want to know the truth about it, I'll tell you I'm gonna *hold* on to it . . ."

This is a quintessentially female record. Indeed, the piano riff that dominates it (played by Aretha, I think; the arrangement is certainly hers, from start to finish; she didn't write the song, but, like Billie Holiday before her, she makes it her own, gives it meanings its author never dreamed of) can be heard as a truly (deeply) feminine variation on the Muddy Waters riff that reaches its apotheosis on Bo Diddley's "I'm A Man." Aretha's riff is yielding rather than assertive, but the groove it builds around itself and the statements it makes are just as memorable.

It all comes together, of course, in the chorus, the ways she shouts "never!" and "no no" and then her extraordinarily sultry "loved a man / the way that I / I love you." The texture of her voice throughout the performance could not be re-created by any other singer. The stories she tells and the emotions she's feeling are unique to the person telling them, and that's the point. Love is a specific experience, not a general one. This is not a message song. It's testimony. To testify about one's experience of God usually is a story with a positive ending, faith rewarded. Testifying about one's experience of another human being is more open-ended, and to be fully honest must finally exist outside of the realm of judgment. Is he, is this relationship, good or evil? There is no answer, and yet the question stays there. And the pain is so real.

What an amazing art form this is! Oh that voice. "You're no good," she says as the record opens, and right away my response is pure contradiction. I'm grateful. I feel nourished. The power of her presence is awesome. I feel myself being given life.

*First release:* Atlantic 2403, February 1967

# 47 Smokey Robinson and the Miracles

## *The Love I Saw in You Was Just A Mirage*

Now you see it, now you don't. And the deceiver is not the other person, though he or she naturally bears the brunt of our accusations, but love itself. Here's Smokey Robinson again, with one of his favorite messages: things are seldom what they seem. He acts it out, his protagonist a deceived suitor (she wasn't really interested in him; can there be a graver insult?), kind of a complainer really, a crybaby, but that goes with the territory. The language of his complaint sparkles from the start, reaching a brilliant crescendo in the song's closing image: "Just like the desert shows a thirsty man/A green oasis where there's only sand/You lured me into something I should have dodged—" The second time through this verse fades to an end right here, leaving the song's unspoken title phrase echoing in the mind of the listener. "Just a mirage." Record's over, but we still hear that lovely (haunting) bass-and-harpsichord figure that would have followed the chorus, we're still entranced by the mysteriously affirmative (ecstasy of pain) "oooooooh-yeaahhh" Smokey breathed before repeating the final verse. Listen to me one last time now. The record discusses and illustrates the transitory nature of pleasure, and its inevitable replacement by loss. Now you hear it, now you don't.

This is what we treasure about singles, about this form of musical art—the quickness with which the song ends, the way it leaves us wanting more, wanting to go back into it, wanting to hear it again. Sweet connection.

It's a two-part experience. The first part is you hear the song on the radio. The second part is you form a connection with it, a bond, waiting impatiently to hear it again, calling to request it, ultimately going to the store and buying a copy so you can play it whenever you want. It's your record now, has been since the first time you realized you liked it a lot. In a sense this bonding comes *after* you hear the song, as well as during; it comes when you start to feel its absence. "Just a minute ago your love was here . . ." Something's missing. That's when you notice you're in love.

I love this record. I love the sound of the words, the sound of the voice, the sound of the drums, the aching transcendence (moment of breakthrough) in the instrumental break. Another single—I'm thinking of the Beatles' "Strawberry Fields Forever"/"Penny Lane," released the same month—may be far richer, more complex, more profound, may seem to have much more to offer me, but in the end beauty is based on feeling rather than reason, and that single for all its glories wears on me quickly, I can't listen to it over and over, whereas this one gives me pleasure, excites me, stirs up my feelings more and more the more I listen, there's just something about the way its elements come together that speaks to *what I need.* And my response is, I hear it as beautiful. I inhale it. I long for it, play it in my mind when it's not on the phonograph. I miss it, and pleasure in it when it's restored to me. I want more.

It's an illusion, I know. This record doesn't love me back, and the singer doesn't even know I exist, except under the general heading of "customer," "audience." But I don't mind. I have my piece of plastic and my device for getting sound out of it, and when I put them together something rich and satisfying flows in through my ears and fills every cell in my body. Over and over. Every time. A very reliable illusion. Fleshly love should only be so constant.

*First release:* Tamla 54145, February 1967

# 48 The Kinks

## *Waterloo Sunset*

The richness of life. That's what this record's about, which is to say, that's what music is about, at its best, when it is most pleasing, most nourishing, most reassuring, most exciting. Music is about fullness, brimfulness, cup running over, fullness to bursting. It is about the happiness (and sadness) of the open heart. It is about how much we are able to feel when we allow ourselves to feel. And "Waterloo Sunset" is one of those perfect little songs and performances that fully provides what most of us most want from music: stimulation, illumination, beauty, friendship. It is one of the great healing rock and roll recordings, in a class with "Don't Worry Baby" and "Here Comes the Sun."

It was a #2 record in England, but in America it didn't even make the top 100. So it goes.

How does it heal? This is really a mystery. I thought I knew the answer back in the fall of '67, when my young life had gotten out of control in a number of ways, and every now and then I would find myself overcome by an irrational (no obvious proximate cause) paralyzing fear, a condition so intense and painful that just the hint that I might be about to feel it again would throw me into a panic. I had to find a way to relax that would work for me at those moments, a method of intervention to slow and stop the onrushing terror after I first caught a glimpse of it and before it overwhelmed me completely. The litany from Frank Herbert's novel *Dune,* "Fear is the mindkiller," was helpful to me, mostly I think because it let me know I was not alone in having to deal with this situation. For the same reason I found tremendous comfort in the implicit confession of the singer (Ray Davies and/or a fictional character he's created) of "Waterloo Sunset" when he says, "And I won't/Feel afraid/As long as I gaze on/Waterloo sunset/I am in paradise . . ." I could call on that comfort, once I'd identified it, by remembering the song's existence and letting a bit of its music run through my mind whenever the fear started to stir, and it helped, it helped a lot. I thought that what helped was the singer's courageous acknowledgment that he, too, felt great fear, for no apparent reason, and had had to find ways to come to terms with it. I appreciated his willingness to share that with me. I believed that that was what was helping and healing me.

I was right, but only half right. Because—and this is the mystery—what was also calming and strengthening and supporting me was something beyond concept and lyric content, something directly transmitted by (the memory of) the music.

It's true that the song's about paralysis. This guy has an apartment in the middle of London, overlooking the dirty Thames and the crowded streets in front of the train station, he sees the young lovers (Terry and Julie, names inspired by Terence Stamp and Julie Christie, who were starring in a film of Hardy's *Far from the Madding Crowd*), but he can't go out to be one of them ("I am so lazy, don't want to wander, I stay at home at night"). So he watches through his window instead. And he's happy—a happiness not diminished but seemingly heightened by his awareness and acceptance of his agoraphobic condition.

In the breach, this individual—putting all irony aside—has at least momentarily found the meaning of life. We know this because we can hear it. That's the mystery. The beauty of the singing, lead and background both, the exquisite and unique richness of the melody and rhythms and harmonics of this performance, the perfection, for example of the lead guitar sound and the tambourine/snare accompaniment, the timing of every element of the song, all these things work together to convey a feeling and a truth that is anything but trivial and certainly could never be contrived. We hear it. We feel it. And we are filled by it.

This is what music is about: direct transmission of the most profound secrets of the human heart. This is the source of its healing power. The singer's undisguised anxiety, his fiercely imaginative and intuitive songwriting techniques, the beauty of his voice and the brilliance of his band's supporting performance, all these things open the door. But what comes through at rare moments like this one is beyond any possibility of explanation. The only word for it is grace.

*First release:* Pye 7N 17321 (U.K.), April 1967

# 49 The Doors

## The Crystal Ship

To me it's a classic juke box song, the B-side of a big hit single ("Light My Fire"), musically and lyrically a mood piece all the way, it just fills the room with attitude, texture, pose, romantic wasted nihilism and cool adolescent snottiness, tug-at-the-heartstrings larger-than-life I-am-sexy voice, drug references, subtle humor, outrageous bullshit, the whole nine yards. And of course being a B-side it has a certain cachet, people expect you to punch up the hits, you gotta dodge 'em, come in from another direction, show that you know where the magic's hidden, demonstrate that you're hip. This song projects the essence of the Doors' mystique: ominous, seductive, decadent, ultimately shallow yet strangely enduring. It's already apparent that Jim Morrison (aided by some chart success and an early death) successfully invented a persona for himself that won't quit, like Verlaine and Rimbaud before him he lives eternally the role of dark poet, beautiful self-destructive visionary. He was a great stage performer before his alcoholism and fame took their toll, an inconsistent songwriter and recording artist, and a rather mediocre poet. He was a sex symbol who delivered little (according to women who knew him), but—after all—in a symbol it's the promise that counts. Reality is a quickly passing phenomenon, but appearances last forever.

Appearances. We could say this song appears to be about a mystical journey but is actually about taking amphetamine ("crystal"), but it would probably be more accurate to say it appears to be about shooting meth but is actually about a mystical journey. What is clear is that the singer is talking to someone, presumably a woman, and that he is leaving her to go on this journey (taking another hit of speed) and mocking her for her reluctance to join him ("Deliver me from reasons why you'd rather cry; I'd rather fly"). He is, like many a romantic poet before him, making the case for his way of living/dying.

But notice two things: that there's no love in him for this person he's speaking to (tenderness, yes; but a dog with sad eyes beside the dinner table is also tender) . . . and that he sincerely equates freedom with traveling on this crystal ship.

This is sad. It can also be very enticing. And this leads to a question: what is the moral standard (if any) for rock and roll? (Did the Village People's "YMCA" encourage unwise sexual practices?) What is the moral standard for any art? There's an answer, I think, and it's brief (though not simple). The answer is: tell the truth.

And the triumph of "The Crystal Ship," what gives it its enduring power, is that it very much does tell the truth about a certain state of mind, a state of mind that is central to what rock and roll is about (to its listeners) and, for that matter, to what in large part the contemporary world is about, at least in what I like to call the overdeveloped countries.

This state of mind has two names, which at first glance have nothing to do with each other, but which are in fact two sides of the same feeling: the names are, "loneliness" and "Party!" These are not bad things. They are central to the rites of passage of all adolescents. At the peak of this rite of passage (which to some extent is an ongoing process in each of us, whatever our age), there is an arrogance that says, "This is the only real adventure, the only worthwhile pursuit." This is not just a justification for self-indulgence and avoidance. It is also, paradoxically, a summoning of courage.

The song only seems to be about having a good time, and sneering at the faint of heart.

What it's actually about is jumping into the abyss.

*First release:* Elektra 45615, May 1967

# 50 The Beach Boys

## *Heroes and Villains*

This is it. This is the record I love better than and indeed am more awestruck at than "Good Vibrations" (less perfect, but it goes so much further). In fact, if I had arranged this book in the foolish (but popular) hierarchical format, this record is one of the few that could have been a legitimate contender for first position. Right up there with "Mona." That tells you something, but damn if I know what.

Oh, actually, I suppose I do know what. Both are totally individualistic and at the same time alarmingly close to some kind of truly universal, pure human essence. In "Mona" it's the rhythms, and the singer's voice. In "Heroes and Villains" it's the rhythms of the voices, and of all the other sounds (voices of another sort). "Mona" is a single voice, speaking from deep in the under-conscious; "H & V" is a collective vocalization, speaking from the same deep place. Both have for me the unmistakable sizzle of a direct hook-up with higher awareness. Here is a taste of what reality really sounds like. Pipes of Pan. The voice of the avatar.

But don't let me spook you. It's a real pretty record, that's all. Astonishingly pretty. The words were written by a fellow named Van Dyke Parks, chosen by him for their sounds the way a mosaicist chooses stones for color and shape and relation to each other and magical resonance and then puts them together and they make a story, a picture. "I've been in this town so long that back in the city I've been taken for lost and gone and unknown for a long long time . . ." This is not mediocre poetry. Even if it weren't surrounded by such wonderful music, it'd be exquisite.

"Heroes and Villains" sounds, among other things, like a running brook. It sounds like nature looks and sounds and smells when we are in it and are truly in touch with the wonder of the natural world. It flows and dances. And, as that last word suggests, there is also a strong element of fantasy here. I am talking now not of the story but of the images conjured up by the music and by the sounds of the performance. As in "A Midsummer Night's Dream" we are caught up in the easy shift from the rapturously natural to the supernatural—"heroes and villains" because this is storybook stuff, a dance to the feelings evoked in a child's heart by the world of make-believe.

This record is a famous failure, in terms of its creators' impossible ambitions: it was to be the cornerstone of an evocative masterpiece that would have taken the sounds and feelings and wordplay explored herein, and extended them across a coherent album-length work, as complex and rich and perfect as anything ever attempted in composed or recorded music. Many additional fragments of "Heroes and Villains" exist on tape that may someday be released in their unfinished form. I'd love to hear them, and I love this legend of the album (called *Smile*) that flew too close to the sun. But the brightness of the myth can obscure what was in fact accomplished. All great works of art are failures in the sense that they reach for something that is ultimately beyond expression. It is not enough simply to reflect back the world that's known. What we love in art is the way it articulates and glorifies our own secret struggles to know and possess the unknowable.

We are most human, most mortal, when we are reaching for something. And though we will never obtain what we reach for, our vulnerability at these moments of hyperextension is a gateway through which the most wondrous possessions can and do arrive. In "Heroes and Villains," the single Brian Wilson did have the courage and humility to complete and release in the form in which we know it, the one now playing on my phonograph, something comes to life that I have never heard on any other recording. Its presence is most obvious in the chorus ("Heroes and villains, just see what you've done done") as it moves from vocalization of words to vocalization of sound to nonvocal sound and back again, and in the violent, breathtaking transitions in and out of this chorus and indeed between all the perfectly integrated and overlapping fragments of this record.

What is that something? Damn if I know. But I know where you can find it.

*First release:* Brother 1001, July 1967

# 51 Van Morrison

## *Brown Eyed Girl*

I was going to say this is a song about sex, and it is, and a song about youth and growing up, and memory, and it's also —very much and very wonderfully—a song about singing. What a great performance! Such easy, happy music, guaranteed to brighten the heart and bring a smile absolutely every time you hear it, something Latin in the rhythms, fabulous bass solo break in the middle, Van's voice so open and radio friendly, ears hear and the body lilts a little in invariable dancing response.

But the words. They sneak up on you, so deftly underplayed, slipped into this delightful pop confection, just words, you know, to carry the tune, "hey where did we go—" and then later it hits you, the poignance, loss, sweet-sadness and overflowing love of life carried haiku-like in every phrase, starting at the beginning, "Hey, where did we go?" indeed. Good question. By implication it's a twenty-year-old looking back at seventeen, but you know it's not a feeling that gets old, just as poignant at any moment in life when you fall into the mood to "cast my memory back there Lord/Sometimes I'm overcome thinkin' about," in the whole history of rock and roll I'm not sure teenage lovemaking has ever been more perfectly captured or more lovingly celebrated, you can feel the touch of the flesh though he says nothing about it, feel it as it feels in his memory, our memory, just as good you know and in some ways better, it hurts, it's so good, linger on, lingers on.

"So hard to find my way, now that I'm all on my own . . ." Yeah. "Whatever happened to Tuesday and so slow?" Donna answered the question for me and the whole song fell into place. "They grew up." Yes. They did.

But of all these wonderful wonderful words that emerge so slyly from the charming skip and jump of the music, the best and most powerful are an aside, a little vocal interpolation at the peak of the bridge, and what a bridge: "Do you remember when, we used to sing—sha la la la la la la la la la la te dah (just like that)?" Just like that. Singer points a finger at the singing and tells us something we maybe didn't know, didn't remember: sex is singing. Youth is singing. This is it. And (cast my memory back there notwithstanding) it's here. It's happening right now.

I'll keep it short this time. There's nothing more to say. Just one more perfect irreplaceable all-time great rock and roll record, breathe it in and let it go. And oh yeah. I was going to say. A song about love.

*First release:* Bang 545, July 1967

# 52 Jackie Wilson

## (Your Love Keeps Lifting Me) Higher and Higher

To a live performer, a hit single has one great significance: it brings work. One hit, and you're in demand; a handful of hits, and some talent to back them up, and you've got a career. Whatever money a record makes tends to come and go pretty quickly, but regular work is something else: it means you can keep making music and keep eating, both, and that's usually all a performer asks for, other than the audience's attention. Jackie Wilson, who had fourteen top 10 rhythm & blues hits between 1958 and 1970, six of them also in the pop top 10, was, according to all reports, very very good at getting and holding a live audience's attention. The Apollo Theater billed him as "Mr. Excitement."

A hit single can also mean playing the same song at every show for the next twenty years or the duration of your life, whichever is longer. Putting a positive face on it, a hit provides a bridge between audience and performer, a basis on which to begin to build a relationship.

But the performer exists (starves, maybe, but exists) with or without the hit record. What I'm getting at is that for many musical and vocal artists, the live stage is their creative home, the place where their highest artistry is found and expressed. They don't go on tour to promote their records so much as they make records in an attempt to capture a little of the magic of their live performance on disc. A single is an opportunity to take what is already there between performer and audience and try to extend it to an unseen audience, to take the heat of one's stage show and radiate it so it can be felt thousands of miles away (and on a thousand different nights) across the airwaves.

Jackie Wilson is no longer alive, but some small part of the specialness of his stage presence, his act, his art, does live on in this record. It's the way he *gets into it.* Against an irresistible rhythmic backdrop (joyous unrelieved tension all the way) he delivers this clever song with the passionate energy of a country preacher high on God, giving every word out of his mouth a velocity and personality and indeed consciousness all its own. Emphasis. The performer, feeling a connection with his audience as immediate as that between two lovers, shares his presence and communicates the intensity of his feeling by emphasizing words as he sings them, touching, caressing, reassuring, arousing—so awake, so alive, he stimulates his listener/partner to a state of heightened awareness, sensitive to the touch and content of every spoken syllable. This is literally an altered state, comparable to the effect of psychedelic drugs or alcohol or good preaching or good loving. The uptempo rhythmic drone (as the song begins we hear the two basic figures that combine into the rhythm track come in one at a time, and somehow the effect is delightful, hypnotic, riveting) awakens and holds our physical awareness and allows the singer to liberate and interact with our deeper, spirit side. The sound of his voice as he urgently articulates "lifting," shouts "higher," and then exhales "keep on" in a transcendent falsetto burst (with a wonderful split-second growl of satisfaction at the end of the two-syllable epiphany) (second chorus—barely audible—try listening on headphones) penetrates through to the spirit presence in each of us, freeing it (her) to come out and dance and play.

He gets into it, and so we get into it. That's the performer's gift. This single contains it, radiates it, immortalizes it. Lyrically, it also acknowledges and celebrates the role the live audience plays, tells us what we do for the performer. Keep lifting him. Higher and higher. We get into it, and so he gets into it. Our presence, our attention, is our love.

*First release:* Brunswick 55336, August 1967

# 53 The Who

## *I Can See for Miles*

This is a song about jealousy and rage. The feelings it expresses are violent ones, and that violence is successfully captured and given voice in the music, slashing guitar chords and drums like windows shattering when attacked by fist or foot. The image of Pete Townshend stalking the stage during a performance of "My Generation," swinging his guitar like a two-headed axe, knocking down the mike stands and then actually slamming his guitar into the amps, venting real frustration, real hatred, including (paradoxical) hatred of the phoniness of having to repeat this stunt night after night, finally breaking the body of the guitar in two in a series of orgasmic assaults on the stage floor, tossing the pieces aside or into the audience, walking off with a look of disgust, still angry—this image recurs in all the instrumental passages of the Who's great singles, but never more vividly than in "I Can See for Miles." There's an enormous smoldering power here that goes, I think, rather beyond nihilism—more than a random hitting out in all directions, or pulling the building down on your own head—rather a horrible concentrated Knowingness, wide-awake focused fury unable to find a victim worthy of its attention, Ahab working himself up, wishing only that he believed in God enough to spit in the old bastard's face, or, indeed, drive a harpoon into him. But he doesn't; I mean, young Townshend doesn't. So he just shouts out the feeling of it all instead, he and Moon and Daltrey and Entwistle shout it into the air with incredible smugness and confidence and, underneath the mask, an astonishing absence of hope.

Other times I hear this as an assertion of life, a visionary proclamation. "I can see for miles." A hymn to clarity and farsight.

What does clarity have to do with rage? Everything, of course. Clarity is the exaltation of the ego, dread intoxication of the perception system. We're all assholes when we think we know what's going on.

And yet rage is healthy. It is a choosing of life. It is the opposite of resignation. It is an appropriate response to feelings of jealousy, a life-affirming reply to the imagined indifference of the world or the loved one. Scream. Do not go gentle!

The purpose of art is to say, I am. The essence of a great song is the expression and affirmation of a particular feeling: I am here. This is what I sound like. Judge me any way that you care to, but do not deny that I exist. Do not deny it, damn it! "I know you've deceived me, now here's a surprise—" It's sung calm and confident, but just under the surface there's a trembling fury, and it erupts through the guitars and drums: Take that. And that. Faces of our enemies appear, even though we believe we're singing to a loved one. In jealousy, the loved one and the enemy become one and the same, actually, viscerally. We blow out our circuits. Lose our senses. Violence, our taboo, our fascination: "Well here's a poke at you, you're gonna choke on it too, you're gonna lose that smile—" This language would be unsuitable for the radio, were it not that the poke is clearly a verbal one, in the form of information, the knowledge that "all the while, I can see for miles and miles . . ." Clearly verbal, but this from a band that actually breaks up its equipment at the end of a show. Not middle class. Fights in the clubs. Fights in the streets outside the clubs. Too much booze. Too little hope.

It's a great record. Whatever makes you angry, here's a meaningful response. Get inside it. Embrace your righteous clarity, illusory though it may be ("the Eiffel Tower and the Taj Mahal are mine to see on clear days"), and own it. Feel it. Live it. Rage. "*Miles* and *miles* and *miles* and *miles* and—" Kick over the drum set. Destroy your guitar. Scream. Maybe you feel better, maybe you don't. It doesn't matter. You're making your statement. Play it again till you feel complete. Bang your head against the wall. This is a way of not going on with the bullshit. It's also a way of deciding to go on with your life.

*First release:* Decca 32206, September 1967

# 54 Otis Redding

# *(Sittin' on) The Dock of the Bay*

Otis Redding knew. Let's not say he knew he was going to die three days after making this record, rather he knew this was his chance for immortality, knew as he laid down this vocal track that it would survive him and be an extension of him, whispering in ten thousand ears, extending the flickering candle of his presence far beyond his mortal reach in both space and time. He knew it, you can hear it. Of course that was the way he was, the way he sang, you can hear it just as sure in each climactic syllable of "I've Been Loving You Too Long (to Stop Now)" on his *Live in Europe* record, he wasn't thinking about the live album they were making, just feeling the audience in front of him, but he knew—knew this was his moment, his one chance to reach these people, to be with them in a way that would stay with them, put something of Otis into their lives, forever. That voice. Makes you shiver. Makes you aware of your breath as it enters your body, and as it leaves again. Otis felt it, felt and lived and expressed in song the not-to-be-repeated opportunity that the present offers. This is it. Here we are. Doing nothing. Except being together.

What a message.

"(Sittin' on) The Dock of the Bay" is about being alone and doing nothing, relaxing, resting, letting go, watching the tide roll in and out. It's actually a kind of protest song, a declaration of independence, self-reliance. The greatest tyrant in the life of a productive person is the sense of obligation, that voice inside (often stimulated or echoed by voices outside) that says, "You're not doing enough, there's important work you should be taking care of, stop wasting valuable time!" The name of this tyrant is guilt—guilt about time—and the unique power of this song is that it both demands and demonstrates freedom from guilt. And the immediate result, tangible to both singer and listener, is contentment, happiness.

"I have nothing to live for, look like nothing's gonna come my way" and "This loneliness won't leave me alone" are not cheerful lyrics, and indeed one could make a reasonable argument, reading the lyrics, that this song's a description of the paralysis depression brings. But even if this is so, no one who actually hears the record can miss the joy expressed in the melody and in the singing. This is, again, a song of healing. It addresses the topics of guilt and depression without denying their power; but from its opening lines ("sittin' in the morning sun, I'll be sittin' when the evening come") what it communicates unflinchingly (not in words but in sound, most of all the sound of the singer's voice) is quietude and liberation.

Liberation! "Look like nothing's gonna change" is hardly a phrase to lift one out of one's funk, but listen to how this climactic bridging verse is sung. No cheerleading (pretty amazing, considering Otis was the king of "gotta, gotta"). No encouragement, no hustle, no effort to turn darkness into light or find the silver lining—none of the phony joyousness that, in situations like this, just deepens the soul's resistance. And, on the other side of the ledger, absolutely no self-pity. Instead, an openness and a self-honesty that reaches out from singer to listener and just vibrates with aliveness, acceptance, relief. "I can't do what ten people tell me to do, so I guess I'll remain the same." And it's all right. More than all right. It's the very essence of freedom. And what it inspires is joy.

Otis knew. And we all know, at one time or another, we've all had these moments of awakening, which is why we recognize the truth when we hear it expressed. The extraordinary gift that Otis Redding had was the ability to share his presence, his most private self, in the act of performance, and to reach out and demand and get his listeners' intimate participation. And on "(Sittin' on) The Dock of the Bay" he (with the help of the great Steve Cropper, here making his third appearance in this book) transcends his own gift, creating something so simple and so penetrating it really will live forever. Just another record, in the sense that the day we die is just another day. But we keep going anyway. There's nothing else to do. I've been loving you too long to stop now.

*First release:* Volt 157, January 1968

# 55 The Who

## *Magic Bus*

Take m'self too seriously sometimes, y'know—sitting here still questioning whether this sloppy, off-key performance with its ridiculous subject matter (guy in love obsessing on the bus that takes him to his girlfriend's house) is absolutely for sure a "100 best" single, worth leaving "Pictures of Lily" "My Generation" "Call Me Lightning" on the cutting room floor for. As if, finally, it made a difference—which it does, to me. The problem is simple: I'm basing my choice on my memory of several different times in my life, years or decades apart, when, listening to "Magic Bus" on headphones, I suddenly started screaming at the top of my lungs (no one around, no inhibitions), just letting it out, what I dunno, didn't even know it was in me, cathartic, overpowering, unforgettable. Making this one of a handful of records on the list that's genuinely pushed me over the top, some kind of satori, what rock is really about, life's high points, and more than once . . . how I could I leave it off? And certainly a marvelous recording in any case. But problem is, you see, I've been listening to the old boy over and over for maybe a week now, and I guess I was expecting somewhere along the line to crack open again. Hasn't happened. Bottom line I guess is if I can't reexperience the scream I can't write from inside of it, 'n I'm hamstrung by my desire to get back to that place and shout at you from the black joyous heart of it. Probably why I'm not satisfied with my write-up on "Gloria," either. Self-importance. Here are songs that have absolutely blown me apart at times. I want to share, demonstrate, show off, maybe even re-create on the page that white heat. Such ambition. Okay. But my listening's not coming through for me, probably 'cause the element of surprise is missing, I'm too hungry, want it too bad, sometimes it has to sneak up on you. I'm trying to get surprised and at the same time keep my eyes cracked open so I can see it coming and figure out how it does that to me, the scientist, you know, then he can explain it, write it down, cover himself with glory. "Can I buy your magic bus?" "Nooooooooh." "I wan' it, I wan't it, I wan' it, I wan' it—" "You can't have it." Jeez.

Rock and roll's first job is to free the child within. Get a beat going and he/she starts moving with it, comes out to dance and play. This motion is important. It stirs things up. And when you get the beat just right—something accomplished partly by the performer, partly by the listener, and partly by the circumstances of the moment, circumstances beyond the control of artist or appreciator but great art does have ways of anticipating circumstances, tuning itself to pick up and amplify the unseen emotional currents that vibrate through our daily lives, lying in wait to be uncovered and resonated with—get the beat just right and it stirs the unknown and unknowable, the underconscious, terror, revelation, joy. Starting with an involuntary movement of head, shoulders, back, as we nod to the rhythm, maybe sway back and forth, from the hips, the child can feel it and starts to come forward ("Too much! It's a magic bus!"—has there ever been a sillier chorus, croaked in voices that would have been sent home from even the most open-minded choir rehearsal?), something is engaged here, dumb as patty-cake but achingly close to the profound mystery of what gives music its power, a question no more likely to be resolved meaningfully than the question of sexual power, I mean, really, mature and intelligent and experienced as we are, how is it we can still be turned (sometimes inside out) by a pretty face? Or a bouncy tune? Go figure.

Notice the acoustic guitar. If the beat's the source of the power and mystery, notice that it ain't the drums or anything electric that originates the beat, or sustains it, or (in this case) articulates its apotheosis (you know, comes back in at just the right moment, provoking our scream). Fingers on stretched strings, rhythmic strum. Heart of the beast. I can feel it. It's starting to get to me. Any moment now—

*First release:* Decca 32362, July 1968

# 56 Jimi Hendrix Experience

## *All Along the Watchtower*

So if the earnest strumming of an acoustic guitar is the primary source, inspiration point, for rock's rhythmic excitement—and I think it is—what's an electric guitar for? The answer, of course, is *sound,* and nowhere is that answer more obvious than in the music of Jimi Hendrix. In 1966/67, with the Beatles and the Stones working to expand the possibilities of rock and roll sound by introducing new instruments, Hendrix came along and expanded those possibilities more strikingly and with more lasting impact than any of his contemporaries by reinventing the instrument that was already there. Electric guitar, phase II. Welcome the Other. This is not black music. It is certainly not white music. Not a clever or even brilliant incorporation of eclectic material or avant garde ideas into familiar pop/rock/folk structures. Nossir. This is a new sound under the sun, obviously and inescapably Something Else, from first listen till the very end of time. Jimi Hendrix's music, especially his guitar-playing, takes off in directions other folks can't even point toward.

"Seen a shooting star tonight, and I thought of you." All lives are brief, some briefer than others, and in this little corner of eternity known to us as the second half of the twentieth century a hit single is an effective way of making some nonharmful noise, proclaiming and calling attention to one's existence, telling whoever in the world may be listening that you have lived and that this fact makes a difference. The light flashes and is gone. But put enough of yourself into that light and it may just burn with a color seldom or never seen, something haunting and awakening, not soon forgotten by those who witness. In this way we beat the clock, if only slightly. In this way we express our desire to join the screaming that comes across our sky.

Two Hendrixes, forever yoked, scream their presence through this record: one personified as the most animate guitar that ever deigned to talk to you or me, and the other, equally powerful but so simple we fail sometimes to notice its impact, his human voice. Jimi twice. Each colors and intensifies the other, flirting and fighting, communicating a complex and extraordinary interdependence, constantly exchanging roles, set and ground, fire and fuel. All framed and supported by the genius of Noel Redding's bass playing, Mitch Mitchell's drums, Bob Dylan's song structure and vision and imagery. The scene is set. A reality captured, constructed. Brilliant preparation. And then Jimi begins to howl.

With a spectroscope we can read the colors in the light of distant suns and learn new truths about our universe. This 45 from another planet offers similar possibilities. Play it loud.

*First release:* Reprise 0767, August 1968

# 57 Grateful Dead

## *Dark Star*

In music we travel. Not from here to there, but from here to out there—and back again. The Grateful Dead launched their career by serving as house band at the Trips Festivals, public group LSD adventures back when the stuff was still legal, and they have never lost their original concept of the purpose of rock and roll: get launched. go out there. hang out. have a good time. see god. come home safely.

"Shall we go/You and I while we can?" This wonderful single is a true fan's delight, an A-side not included in the album of the same era (*Anthem of the Sun,* their second and most psychedelic), perfect two-and-a-half-minute distillation of everything the band was striving to achieve at the time, which is lots. I know of only one group that ever put out a similar-sounding rock single: the Doobie Brothers, "Black Water," a radically eclectic B-side that turned over and became a #1 record. "Dark Star" itself never hit the charts. But it has had its impact.

It has had its impact as one of the more legendary live performances of the most consistently popular live rock and roll band ever. But that's not why it's in this book. It's in the book for the same reasons as all these other records: originality, power, enduring appeal. Transcendence. Endless source of joyous stimulation. The more I listen, the better it sounds.

In music we travel. We want motion, but more than that: we want to go somewhere. The basic structure and essential nature of a Grateful Dead performance is epitomized by two classic tracks from their first album, "Morning Dew" and "Viola Lee Blues": a provocative lyric invocation, a long instrumental improvisation implicitly exploring emotions and images stimulated by the opening verse, characterized by great pioneering outbursts of individualism that are then acknowledged by the rest of the band and transformed into the leading edge of a group voyage, collective expression, peaking, climaxing, turning gracefully and suddenly like a rocket dropping back to earth, usually back to a repetition of the opening verse, now serving as completion, fulfillment, benediction. We went out there. We came home again.

"Dark Star" as a single is a compact variation on this, evoking the magic journey in the breach. It goes out and doesn't come home again. It is a quintessential, impassioned expression of the psychedelic (and human) desire to break through to another universe, through the dark star, into unimaginable wonders; to evolve; to make the leap. Not to go and come back, but to grow and never return. This is the paradox, the emotional deepening, the source of the tension. We feel the excitement of the breakthrough, the transcendent journey, the return to something higher and long forgotten or dimly remembered —but we also feel the loss, feel it as a great longing to swim home to where we started from this morning, balanced against the great longing to swim home to where we've never been in this lifetime, this consciousness, this epoch. The journey out is also a break with all that's kind and warm and familiar. It takes real courage. We look to our group for support. We lead the way with brilliant bursts of individuality even as we helplessly, joyously follow the spirit of the times, of the moment. We call to worship. We make the lonely collective leap into the great unknown.

"Shall we go/You and I while we can?" Gee, I don't know. I can't quite understand what they're saying. But the music sounds so good . . . Wow, here we go. My God, what's that up ahead?! We're going to crash—

*First release:* Warner 7186, August 1968

# 58

## The Beatles

# *Hey Jude*

Inspiration. If there is anything wondrous in the human universe to compare with sunsets and mountain ranges and dew on the leaves, it is to be found in our inspired expressive creations, one of the great examples of which is this recorded performance. I'm not one of the Beatles' most loyal admirers, but "Hey Jude" kicks ass on a par with Van Gogh or Beethoven in their prime. It is, let's say, one of the wonders of this corner of creation, twentieth-century Western world.

What is it? A song, a tune, a record, a performance. What's that? A way of combining music and words in a moment of creative activity partially planned yet wildly spontaneous, in front of an audience keenly felt even if unseen, delivering them loudly into the open air via voice and percussion and amplified instruments. A shout. A melody. A thing in motion. A measurable thing with a start and finish, seven minutes and eleven seconds long in this case, shelvable, replayable, and yet for all the specificity of its start and end a thing that is infinite or anyway supernaturally indefinite in its middle. It opens out like the sky at night or the idea of the existence of God.

Inspiration. The song has a front and a back and a thin, miraculous transition connecting them. The song's idiosyncratic structure (quick! name even one other piece of music that's built like this) is startlingly regular: there are six four-line verses in the front half, four "standard" and two "bridging" (an alternate melody and rhythm that neatly plays off the first, providing relief and excitement, and that, in most songs, serves as a "middle eight" bridge between similar front and back sections). All of the "standard" verses begin "Hey Jude, don't—" and end ". . . make it better." All of them have exactly the same metrical structure: six syllables in line one, nine in line two, ten in line three, nine in line four. All have an internal rhyme connecting the end of the third line ("heart," "skin") with the middle of the fourth ("start," "begin"). The bridging verses mirror each other similarly, twelve beats ten beats twelve beats ten beats, internal rhyme between the middle of the third line and the end of the third. The one irregularity is that the second and fourth lines of the second bridging verse don't rhyme at all ("perform with," "shoulder"). The transition out of these sweet, regular, extremely powerful front verses comes with the sudden repetition of the last word of the standard verse, "better." The singer goes up the ladder with this word, breaking the universe open with a deceptively soft scream ("ahhhhh!") as he reaches the top of his ascent, descending again just as suddenly ("yeah yeah yeah yeah yeah yeah") (the "better"s recall *Sgt. Pepper,* the "yeah"s "She Loves You," but that might be accident) and sliding with breathtaking ease into the stately, euphoric "na-na-na na"s that populate the mind-boggling back section of the performance. This back section consists of nineteen lines. The last fades midway, the first drops three "na"s to connect to the "yeah yeah yeah" bridge, but the other seventeen are precisely the same in terms of form and lyric: fourteen beats, "Na, na na, na-na-na na, na-na-na na, Hey-ey Jude." Against this regularity in both front and back is an inspired, semicontrolled brilliant punctuation consisting of powerful almost subliminal piano/orchestra rhythms, equally powerful irregular out-front drum outbursts, and an unending, irregular, demonic, Dionysian series of screams, violently attacking the calm reassurance of the lead vocal without ever shaking it from its patient path. Some sort of primordial drama is enacted, with more twists and turns and delicious subtleties than can begin to be heard or comprehended—like Paul's quick "Joo-oo-oo-wude" in the last verse of the front section. The component parts of music, of song, of human emotion expressed in sound, are taken apart and gone inside of—let's strip away the illusion of meaning and get down to the na-na-na that underlies it—and put back together again with reckless and thoroughly justified confidence. Ballad is reinvented and married to rhythm in a new sort of union. And so forth and so on. I can't begin to talk about this. How did he think of that astonishing transition? Pure inspiration. Let it out and let it in. A song about breathing.

*First release:* Apple 2276, August 1968

# 59 Marvin Gaye

## *I Heard It Through the Grapevine*

It's hypnotic. The tambourine rattle at the beginning puts us under, and the soft-spoken, relentless rhythm track holds us in trance. The sinuous vocal completes the package. We listen like the snake's victim watching it weave: paralyzed; fascinated; wondering in strange detachment just when the strike will come.

Marvin Gaye, like so many black voices in rock and roll, comes straight out of gospel, and gospel, though its subject matter be Jesus of Nazareth, comes straight out of Africa. Mother of darkness. And my God how we crave and hunger for that darkness in our daily lives! How our ears perk up when we hear it calling.

"I'm just about to lose my mind. Honey, honey, yeah."

Don't actually want to lose it, y'understand. But I am powerfully attracted to any voice that acknowledges and articulates my confusion and pain.

There's a beautiful, unyielding tension in this recording, and also (paradoxically, because it's such a clever product, such a perfectly contrived arrangement) an unmistakable authenticity. What is it we hear? A lot of the time, I guess, we don't have a name for it. But we know immediately when it's for real. It's a feeling that cuts to the bone.

Dum da dum dum, da da dum dum, *dum* da dum dum, da da dum dum . . . Oh that riff. A subtle variation on "Mysterioso," I think. I've seen this movie before. But it still makes my blood run cold.

A good riff gets into the blood, and, in a sense, it comes from the blood as well. What else is the source of our attraction to and fascination with rhythm? Heard it pulse around us (oh mother of darkness) floating in the womb, and it's been pulsing in our ears before and beneath all other sounds ever since.

Music heightens the pulse, heightens our awareness of our rhythmic environment. Heightens the emotional feedback cycle that makes capillaries race or crawl. Feel it, feel it, get into the anger, the vulnerability, the loss, even the grim satisfaction of having uncovered the unwanted truth. Let it circulate. Feel the trembling of the awakened heart. It's not exactly fun. But—in contrast to denial—it gives life.

The song is about suspicion and confrontation. It's about that dangerous moment when suppressed fears are aired, released. We love it for its fabulous sound, its drive, its unremitting intensity. Sweet. Seductive. Penetrating. Hypnotic.

Tambourine at the beginning puts me under, but there's no corresponding rattle at the other end to wake me when it's over. Guess I'll just have to listen again, and again, and again . . .

*First release:* Tamla 54176, November 1968

# 60 The Rolling Stones

## *Honky Tonk Women/You Can't Always Get What You Want*

It should always be like this. The radio says, "Here it is, the new Rolling Stones single," they play it, and it's truly brand new, like nothing you've ever heard before and like everything you've always wanted to hear, condensed down into three exquisite minutes that perfectly define our moment, summation of all human and personal history up to this point. You go to the record store, take it home, and discover the B-side is totally different yet again, and every bit as good.

Stay home for the next two weeks and just soak it in. (Or, alternatively, go on an unplanned adventure, disc of plastic under your arm, ready for anything.)

Some say those days will never come again. But what the hell do they know? They've become the very people who said those days would never come in the first place.

"Honky Tonk Women" has the sound worth waiting lifetimes for. If you're coming to it late, forget the CD. All wrong (1980's pressings anyway). Get it on vinyl—seven-inch far preferable, but an album's all right. Crank it up. Listen to that guitar riff. Now that's what I call *emphasis.* This is, like, a major statement on the quality of experience. This is what it feels like. "Bomp ba Dahhh!" Thank God someone was finally able to articulate it. Secret truth spoken clearly (and in public) always comes as a tremendous relief.

Authority. Here it is again, in a strange new guise. Not "here I am" (as in "Mona") but "here we are"—not an announcement but a declaration, spoken with utter confidence and certainty, you hear it in the group voice that sings "Hah-ah-ah-ahonnnky Tonk *Wo*men," like they don't have the slightest doubt about the information they're imparting (how could they with that guitar riff backing them up?): "This is the way that it is." Yes sir. Yessuh. All right!

A dance-hall song. Bawdy lament. Heavy metal country. "I just can't seem to drink you off my mind." I will keep trying, however.

(It might seem difficult to make these silly lyrics into a brilliant commentary on everything that's going on in the universe, but our ears always find a way.)

On the other side, one of the all-time great footnotes, from the philosopher who attracted his following by observing, "I can't get no satisfaction." Four years later, he offers his much-chewed-on (happier-but-wiser) clarification: "You can't always get what you want—but if you try sometime, you just might find, you get what you need." What does that mean? We know. Oh God, do we know.

And once again, a sound is achieved never heard before or since, rock and roll apotheosis, guaranteed to fill hearts and ears to overflowing and leave us dumbstruck with the wonder of it all. Not guitar this time but Al Kooper's piano and organ and Jack Nitzsche's orchestrated voices, all swooping crescendoes and sweet piano cameos, perfect I mean perfect settings for Mick Jagger's exquisite vocal, not a great singer perhaps when all is said and done but my God he sure did know how to rise to the occasion. A great singer of great singles, just the right tone, right persona, right inflection, so fresh and so present, here and on a double handful of classic 45's left out of this volume, "Jumping Jack Flash" and "Wild Horses" and all those other miracles.

"I saw her today at the reception . . ." The album version is greatly different (two and a half minutes longer) but magically the same. The Stones roll and flow to fit every context. This single encompasses the world in its two sides, says everything these gents could possibly have to say (oh that cowbell), and they still managed to follow it up with probably their greatest album ever. "HTW" reduced to an alternate take, purposely filler, as if to say, "You want the single? Go buy it!" Every moment brand new. Every record the start of something. It should always be like this. Sex and death and humor and attitude and a great beat and guitar piano vocal orchestral rock and roll music to die for.

*First release:* Decca F 12952 (U.K.), July 1969

# 61 Creedence Clearwater Revival

## *Green River*

Return to what? Music seems to know about parts of ourselves that we have hidden from our normal awareness. A guitar-playing friend of mine was telling me how certain chords (or chord changes; the transition is vital) provoke unusual and very powerful responses in us. I know. I can't play the chords, or name them, but I can feel them. I can feel the chemical reactions taking place in my body, my consciousness, my soul. Suddenly I am flooded with an awareness of something I thought I'd lost, coming back to me. My mind thinks it's in the words of the song. My body thinks it's in the rhythm, the pulse. My heart hears the melody, relationships between notes, chord changes (the shifting, all-present background texture out of which melodic foreground emerges?), pitch of voice. My soul hears everything together, no judgment, no differentiation—and responds. "Take me back down where cool waters flow, y'all/da da da da, *da* da da da da da." Singer and guitar and band are putting out words/music the same way my spirit takes it in: all one object, undifferentiated, all notes and sounds and rhythms working together to make a single note, message, feeling. "Let me remember things I done, oh (things I don't know)/da da da da, *da* da da da da da . . ."

> Love to kick my feet way down the shallow water
> Shoe fly, dragon fly, get back to mother
> Pick up a flat rock, skip it across
> Green River—

What is poetry? What does it achieve? If we define great poetry in terms of the strength and nature of its impact on the reader or listener, if we create a language of criticism that is truly descriptive of what happens when eye (not pen) touches page, it follows as the day the night that John Fogerty/

Creedence Clearwater Revival cannot be left off the list of twentieth century masters of the art form. Listen—not to the words on this page but to the sound of the song in your mind or on the record player, notice the extraordinary internal rhymes, onomatopoeia, notice the immediacy (simplicity/complexity) of the visual image before you as you listen, notice sounds, smell, touch of stone, air, water:

Pick up a flat rock, skip it across
Green River—

The third verse is even better. This poem/performance is more than perfect. It would have to be, to achieve such an impact. "Up at Brody's Camp I spend my day . . ." Suddenly, beyond the universality of these wonderfully specific memories of nature and childhood, comes the clear whiff of narrative. Two verses of gloriously tangible images (and the nonverse, instrumental break, which is pure feeling, most evocative poetry of all) are instantly recast as part of a story, and just in time (in the amazing economy of song structure, whole novels in the snap of a finger or blink of an eye) for the moral. And what a moral, climax/anticlimax, koan, something solid enough and ambiguous enough to live with and be nourished by for a lifetime (words printed here just as stand-in for performance, remember):

Old Brody Jr. took me over
Said you're gonna find the world is smould'rin'
And if you get lost, come on home to
Green River—

That's it. You find me a print poem that has more to say about the twentieth century. I dare you. I double dog dare you.

*First release:* Fantasy 625, July 1969

# 62 Velvet Underground

## *Foggy Notion*

Alternate universe time. In some other reality just under the surface of this one, the Velvet Underground were bigger than the Beatles, and "Foggy Notion," despite its six-minute-and-twenty-second length, was #1 for eleven weeks in the fall of 1969. In this reality, however, the Velvets never scratched the top 100 on either side of the pond, despite being the quintessential (and, in the long term, perhaps the most influential) rock and roll band of their era. It's true "Sweet Jane," a rock classic if ever there was one, was released as a 45 at some point in the U.K., but no one noticed and it's not a song I think of as a single, its identity rests somewhere else. "Foggy Notion" on the other hand I first encountered as a slice of seven-inch vinyl, a 45-rpm bootleg issued (reputedly with the tacit cooperation of Lou Reed) in New York City in 1976. To me it's the great Velvets AM radio world saturation essence of rock and roll pure statement of existence hit single that never was. I think they should set up the planet's last record-playing phonograph in the Smithsonian with a copy of "Foggy Notion" on it playing over and over and over through tinny speakers till the turntable rusts or the record wears flat or the barbarians storm the city and destroy all traces of our once-great civilization.

Until then, we dance.

Leaving aside the vaguely sadomasochistic lyrics (no no you don't understand they're just hitting her to make sure she doesn't overdose), this song is sheer white riff. White because unlike most of the other rhythms in rock and roll, this nervous double-time repeating drum figure, and the amazing guitar bursts that dance alongside it, don't seem to have roots in any black American musical traditions I'm aware of. There is some kinship perhaps to Coltrane in his more frenetic moments, but no obvious predecessor. Maureen Tucker on drums, Sterling Morrison on rhythm guitar, and Lou Reed on lead guitar and vocals have in fact created something new under the sun (Doug Yule on bass contributes significantly to the gestalt of this track, but the others were working on the riff years before he showed up), and punk rock and speed metal are probably just the first of many musical genres that will draw from this well in years to come.

It's so simple. "Discoveries of great moment in mathematics and other disciplines," says G. Spencer Brown, "once they are discovered, are seen to be extremely simple and obvious, and make everybody, including their discoverer, appear foolish for not having discovered them before." Maureen is standing in the middle with her mallets, beating out this insistent boom-boom-snap! rhythm over and over with incredible speed and steadiness—a fraction early on the snap! I think is the trick that drives the engine, makes the blood boil in musicians' and listeners' veins. Behind her (aurally) is the bass, supporting the beat at times but also free to solo around, jazz-fashion, commenting on and exploring and deepening the mystery before returning to home base. The two guitars stand on either side of the drum riff, which is really a drum/rhythm guitar riff, Sterling riding the drumbeat with his "broken-down syncopated guitar strumming" (thanks Richard Mortifoglio), Lou presumably responsible for the more lyrical lead guitar excursions, except that when you listen carefully both guitars are playing rhythm much of the time, and either one seems capable of taking off in unexpected "lead" lines, explorations of the narrow but infinite free space dead ahead, the corridor between the hood of the engine and the horizon (rushing closer at every moment, though you know we're never going to get there).

And that's all. Drums in the middle, guitars all around, speed in a straight line (with broken fingerings, creating nervous insistent inventive polyrhythms) from here to the event horizon. And every now and then (according to very rigorous song structure imperceptible to us as we race along with the runners) this music of the spheres is interrupted by astonishing timeless vocal passages, Lou Reed so present, so totally outside of time, laughing, standing still like the hummingbird, doing calisthenics with his voice while the music rushes ever forward. "Well, I've got a foggy notion. All right . . ." And then back to the infinite. "Do it again." "All right." "Do it again." Welcome to the new world. "I've got a foggy notion . . ."

*First release:* "White Heat" bootleg single, 1976; recorded May 6, 1969

# 63 Sly and the Family Stone

## *Thank You (Falettinme Be Mice Elf Agin)*

Scary or reassuring? It depends. Are you hearing the verse ("Looking at the devil, at his gun" "Dying young is hard to take") or the chorus ("Thank you for letting me be myself again")? Or are you hearing the subtle, seemingly unresolvable tension in the transition from one to the other ("We begin to rassle/I was on the top/I want to thank you . . .")? Some critics hear the chorus as sarcastic, and certainly the cute spelling of the song's title suggests a sort of ironic distancing. But from what? Looking back from the vantage point of twenty years later, it's clear that Sly Stone—along with James Brown and very few others—invented the future. Funk, rap, hip hop: it's all here, a radical departure from everything soul music and rock and roll had been, less obvious now only because Motown and the rest of the industry began copying and learning from Sly the instant they heard him. Listen to that talking bass line (fingers slapping guitar strings), not just lead instrument but co-equal with the vocals, shouting out its own message which is separate from verse or chorus and arguably more eloquent (a fact that does not escape the singer/lyricist's attention: "Many things on my mind/Words in the way"). There's a new kind of call-and-response here (introduced in the group's 1968 hit "Dance to the Music") which I believe provokes instant recognition and deep response even in those who did not grow up in the gospel tradition. Something primal is being awakened. This can be scary. And joyous.

The thanks that are offered are sincere. Sly appreciates his audience. But "being myself" has its painful aspects. This song/performance/compilation (Sly is a master of the "kitchen sink" approach) is brilliantly and painfully self-conscious. It is in a sense the opposite of songs like "Dancing in the Street" and "Going to A Go-Go," which captured the energy and spirit of the times without consciously intending to do so. The fierceness of those records is tempered and made possible by their innocence. But in a few short years the rising tide of racial self-awareness has stripped away any possibility of being unaware of one's power and responsibility as a young black man with the ability to influence and inspire a huge interracial audience. Sly seems almost shocked at his power to manipulate—and uncertain what to do with it. The song structure and chorus of "Thank You" belong to a song that is thanking a lover for putting me back in touch with who I really am, reawakening my love for myself . . . a great message, and with this tune and rhythmic structure a natural hit single: surefire. The verses that would support this concept have in effect been erased here, but since we hear what we want to hear it doesn't matter—the record can be received as a powerful, liberating love song, and it did in fact become a #1 hit. Simultaneously, thanks to Larry Graham's bass guitar lines and a great rhythmic feel, the record is also a classic r&b "celebration" dance track, a song about being yourself in the sense of breaking loose and partying and feeling free. Another sure path to the top of the charts. But Sly isn't satisfied. He's an authentically moral man, looking for a way to tell the truth, to integrate the different parts of himself (and his family), to actually be the true self he's singing about.

And as he puts more and more into the song, using the studio (he was a producer before he became a bandleader and performer) with freewheeling grace and astonishing inventiveness, at one point constructing a verse almost entirely of the titles and musical themes of his other hit songs (a scratcher, a DJ, years ahead of his time, playing with and acknowledging the process with a kind of sassiness and flair for paradox that would later be expressed on tracks like M.C. Hammer's "They Put Me in the Mix")—as he throws in all this stuff including overt imagery of the fear and pain and cruelty of life in the ghetto, he does finally succeed (if that's the right word) in expressing the true ambivalence of his achievement of self-rediscovery.

Reality—social or personal—is not always simple, or pretty. "Life is beautiful" and "Life is shit" are easy messages to get across in song . . . unless you find yourself believing both at the same time.

*First release:* Epic 10555, December 1969

# 64 James Brown

## *Get Up I Feel Like Being A Sex Machine (Part 1)*

Not to be outdone. James Brown invented the playground, again and again, opening up vast new realms each time he felt his turf beginning to be encroached on. '50's, '60's, '70's, JB and his influence are everywhere, r&b, soul, funk, and on into the '80's and '90's when the young turks of rap have made him the most sampled man in show business. Simplicity and genius go hand in hand, and what sounds simple may not be, upon closer inspection and taking into consideration the diversity and fierce durability of the Godfather's genes, unto the nth generation. A driven man. Driven to create, express, perform, make money, achieve notoriety, stay in control, and why? Not to be outdone might be the only reason—if you don't stay ahead you could be back to the poverty and powerlessness from which you came, first or last the only choices—or maybe after enough years of driving the driving drives itself, momentum, inertia, but what momentum! Not to stay the same, regardless of how JB's singles might sound to uneducated ears, but to keep ahead. Forward. One silly millimeter at a time, one tiny leap of genius ahead of the pack, forward ("Get up! Get on up"), into the new world.

This record another breakthrough. In context or out of context. Put it on your phonograph. See how it redefines whatever you've been listening to, dancing to, praying to. Relationship. The song has almost nothing to do with sex (except in the basic sense that dancing equals strutting equals sexual expression), but like all music it has everything to do with relationship. I/thou. Lover/loved one. Performer/listener. Conscious self/inner self. "Stay on the scene," James sings, and we know he's speaking to himself, and to the young buck on the dance floor who is the persona in so many of his songs, talking about his relationship with music as the expression of the moment, cutting edge, what's happening now, no fakin', you're either speaking to the new crowd or you're not, "stay on the scene," like he was talking about himself in his 1965 breakthrough single "Papa's Got A Brand New Bag." Dig the new thing. No jive. This is it.

Relationship. This is what? We're down to the real semantic nitty-gritty here, one of the most self-referential recordings ever made, metaphysically ("The way I like it/Is the way it is/I got mine (dig it!)/He got his") and literally: "Bobby!" he shouts at his organist Bobby Byrd, "Should I take 'em to the bridge?" "Go ahead," says Bobby, and of course James repeats himself a few times ("Can I take 'em to the bridge?") and then ("Hit me now!") he gives the signal and the band plays the bridge, changing the hypnotic rhythm figure (played by the guitarist on this song rather than the horn section) for the first and only time in this extraordinary one-chord performance, this music is not like other music, no verse structure, no melody, but rich and full and fully musical in spite of itself, telling us among other things that songs are not what we think they are, they're *performances* and it's the mind of the listener that retroactively receives and interprets them as compositions, anyway, he takes us to the bridge and there we stay, until the fade when he gets the urge: "I want to count it off one more time— You want to hit it like you did on the top, fellas?" and they of course oblige, seven quick horn bursts and back to the basic rhythm just like at the start of the record. The song is about itself. But this is not just cute. It's sincere. It's profound. It's about talking to oneself. It's about singing about life, like we all do inside ourselves, hearing that beat, relating to that beat (my soundtrack), interacting with it, relationship, my relationship with spirit, this is very private stuff, and we speak of it in code: "Get up! (get on up)/Get up! (get on up)/Stay on the scene (get on up)/Like a sex machine (get on up)" . . .

The intention is to induce breakthrough, express breakthrough, demonstrate breakthrough. Transcendence via regularity. The most Apollonian bandleader and (at moments) the most Dionysian singer in pop music (soul, rock, whatever you call it), and they're the same person, and on this single he also plays the piano in the instrumental break, break not bridge, for James at least there's a real distinction. The break is a breather, a chance to catch up, let it start to sink in. The bridge is something else. It's the place he wants to take us to.

Why? Because he always has. Because it's what he knows. Because he can. Because he's got to or die. Because it's the way he likes it. And (this is the sexy part) because it's the nature of our relationship.

*First release:* King 6318, July 1970

# 65 Joe Simon

## *Drowning in the Sea of Love*

It comes in out of the night, maybe while you're driving between cities, or staying in a strange motel listening to the night radio. You hear a song. And you know. You've never heard it before, but you feel it arriving, moving through your body, settling in for a lifetime stay. Hello.

God speaks to us, sometimes, from the radio. And I don't mean the news on the hour. The power of music is it can go right past our everyday considerations and awaken some part of the self that is deep and enduring, touch it and awaken it and momentarily give our conscious minds an awareness of who we really are.

The mystique of the single lies in its wholeness—it is self-contained, an object—and in its otherness. It comes from Out There. It is definable: you can call the radio station and ask to hear it again, you can go to the store and purchase a copy, hold it in your hands. Make it sing to you repeatedly. It becomes familiar, a friend, for a little while at least a very intimate friend, knowing you and touching you in places that are hidden from the eyes of the world. It is an invader, a welcome invader. We requested it, wished for it consciously or unconsciously, when we turned on the radio that night. It responds to a need. Send me something.

We're always surprised when our prayers are answered.

This song washes over me. I like the sound. I like the riff: original, hypnotic, endlessly fascinating like watching waves break on a beach, over and over the same pattern yet still it pulls the attention. Quietness, then the swell, a surge of power, it breaks and breaks and falls inward and begins again. This is not unconscious; the effect has been cleverly orchestrated by two of the sharpest and most professional producer/songwriters in the business, Kenny Gamble and Leon Huff (later known as The Sound of Philadelphia), working with their tightly knit, highly skilled band of studio musicians. But cleverness and professionalism can only take you so far. A record that turns out as great as this one requires more than mere contrivance. There's an X factor, having to do with inspiration, timing, chemistry, luck, "happy accident." Someone somewhere left a door open, and spirit walked into the room.

So simple and so elusive. I love this record. It unlocks something in me, the sound of Simon's voice, the backup singers, the motion of the riff in relation to the song's structure, a timing that causes certain phrases to surge forward and take on special meaning: "a strong wind came into my life," "all I can see/ Is water coming over me," and of course the brilliant refrain: "I've been down one time/And I've been down two times/But now I'm drowning, drowning in the sea of love."

The words of the song are about problems in a love relationship, but what it awakens in me is altogether different: a love for the past, for all the people and places in my life, a feeling of overwhelm and of urgency (a desire to *express* this feeling) and of sweet sad acceptance of the impossible richness of it all. A passion. A kind of surrender, I suppose, and the excitement of that. "I'm drowning"—here I go, it's happening right now, I can feel it—"drowning in the sea of love." The last word is stretched out and I fall back into it. Yet it's not a death but an awakening. It's a very special feeling, and I love the song because, not every time but sometimes, I can listen to it and be absolutely filled with this feeling. It floods out of me. A drowning in reverse.

The song has nothing to do with any place or time (hence my fight against history) except what I as the listener add to it. And that's not done with my conscious mind. The whole process is beyond my control. I turn on the radio, and the song arrives. I buy it, capture it, trap it on my turntable. But the truth, of course, is that it's captured me.

I guess I left the door open. Hello spirit. Welcome to my room.

*First release:* Spring 120, November 1971

66

## The Rolling Stones

# All Down the Line

"Open up and swallow, yeah . . ." This was going to be the lead single off *Exile on Main Street* but at the last moment "Tumbling Dice" got the nod, another very worthy choice (I remember listening to it about a thousand times—"you've got to *roll* me"—holed up in a grungy Tokyo apartment the month it came out), but then just about any track on *Exile* other than "Sweet Black Angel" would have made a great single, don't you think? So "All Down the Line" got missed in the U.K. and came out in the States as the B-side of the second single, "Happy" (Keith's moment in the sun). No matter. I mean, little decisions like this alter the course of rivers and empires and affect millions of lives, but still, no matter. Anyway, next year some dumb but very popular teen movie could come out with this song on its soundtrack (maybe even title theme) and bam, hit record time, ten weeks of total geographical and chronological saturation. All accounts are evened up sooner or later. Time is an illusion. Mass popularity is also an illusion. Ain't nobody here but you and me and our reflection on the wall. Turn on the radio, hon—"Need a shot of salvation, babe, once in a while"—see what I mean? You can't get away from it. Not that it ever really existed in the first place.

What makes "All Down the Line" one of the 100 best rock and roll singles of all time is, uh, its *durability.* Ambiguity plays a role, too. Can't get too specific if you want to be all things to all people. What does "all down the line" mean? I don't know (they also sing "going down the line"). But you can't miss the locomotive rhythms that drive the song from start to finish, from here to that place where the train tracks meet. "You can't say yes and you can't say no/Be right there when the whistle blows" and then a third line that completely escapes me but I love it anyway, in fact perhaps more than I would if I actually could hear what he's saying. And then the guitars and, uh, I'm a very happy kid. Grinning. With my headphones on. I understand the universe. Tell you about it later.

There's nothing more that needs to be said.

*First release:* Rolling Stones RLS 19104, June 1972

# 67

## Bob Dylan

# *Knockin' on Heaven's Door*

"Songs are just thoughts. For the moment they stop time." "Knockin' on Heaven's Door" was written for the soundtrack of Sam Peckinpah's movie *Pat Garrett & Billy the Kid,* to illustrate a scene where a dying sheriff and his wife are saying their last goodbyes. It unexpectedly became a hit single in the fall of 1973, creeping up the charts inch by inch when no one was looking, the way some records do. It's a perfect recording, two verses, two choruses, world-class "ooh-ooh"s at beginning and end and (quieter) all the way through, two minutes and twenty-eight seconds long and wide enough to store a lifetime of feelings in. And thanks largely to the snapshot (a performance captured, preserved, time stopped, moment made eternal) this single is, the song already bids fair to be one of the most-performed compositions of its century. My kids tell me the Guns n' Roses version was the most popular video on MTV last month. A few years ago Bono of U2 introduced the song in concert by saying, "It's taken me seven years to realize that more important than all these amplifiers, more important than this whole building, are these four chords—that's a G, that's a D, I think that's an A-minor, and that's a C. Those four chords mean more than it all, because with those four chords you can write a song, a song like this one."

It's strange, isn't it? Bob Dylan was standing around doing nothing one day (he'd actually been doing nothing for several years at that point), needing one more song fragment for the soundtrack, thinking about this scene in the film, and the song came to him. Probably in a few minutes. His job was to be there, ready to receive it. And he didn't fail.

This is a trance record. It puts you under instantly, I mean instantly, and holds you there lovingly for hours if you just let it play over and over on the phonograph. And if you only hear it once, you'll walk around all day in a half-trance, wondering why the air seems richer and the afternoon light has such an unusual quality. The background voices and the "knock, knock, knockin'" refrain have something to do with this, I'm sure, and the perfect compact imagery of the title and the six short lines (count them) that make up the text of the verses. "Take this badge off of me . . . It's getting dark, too dark to see . . ." Yeah. But mostly what's happening here is that a crack in the universe has opened up. Dylan spotted it lying on a coffee table in the recording studio that day, and picked it up and passed it along to us.

I am staring with my ears into this gap between worlds now. Time is stopped, as Mr. Dylan promised it would be. And as if I myself were about to die, I feel a kind of comradeship with every one else who has been in this place. It's an astonishing feeling.

The song is a prayer, a supplication. Roger McGuinn plays guitar (as does Dylan), Jim Keltner plays drums, Carl Fortina harmonium, Terry Paul bass, and the background singers are Carol Hunter, Donna Weiss, and Brenda Patterson. If you asked one of these people about the session, you'd find that their memories are dim and distant, which seems strange because for you and me that session is right here, in the present, we can feel every corner of the room. Dylan is singing to us now. I'm sure this amazes him as much as anyone. He's still singing the song. Not again, but this one time. Right now. Here on this record.

"To hear a song is to hear someone's thought, no matter what they're describing." And they're still thinking that thought (at least till every last copy of the record has turned to dust). The painter is still looking at the light reflecting from the river. The song is still playing. It gives one pause. And allows one to dance a moment or two longer here before the door swings open.

*First release:* Columbia 4-45913, August 1973

# 68 Bachman-Turner Overdrive

## *You Ain't Seen Nothing Yet*

So it's dumb, so what? Dumb is saintly. Dumb is a relief. Dumb is freedom. In this particular case, dumb is an accident. The story goes that the song was recorded on the spur of the moment as a joke, the three Bachman brothers teasing a fourth brother, their manager, who stuttered. Then came a record company guy, who heard about the gag recording, insisted on hearing it, insisted it be on the album, and later insisted it be released as a single. Songwriter and group leader Randy Bachman resisted at each point, particularly the last. "I refused for three weeks. Then I woke up one day and asked myself, 'Why am I stopping this? Some of my favorite records are really dumb things like "Louie Louie." ' So I said, 'O.K., release it.' "

Dumb is freedom. It's not the stuttering that makes this a great record, it's a certain combination of ingredients, particularly the anthemlike power of the title line, punch line, with its delightful twist of sexual innuendo ("She looked at me with those big brown eyes and said—"), and the marvelously free, unselfconscious, loud crunching right-on-the-money power chords that hammer through the chorus. (There's also a good melody, later stolen for Boston's "More than A Feeling," and yes the stuttering vocal adds charm and makes the silliness of most of the lyrics unimportant or even appropriate.)

Heavy metal fans are called "headbangers" because chords like these make you want to punch the air with your fists—to participate, to be part of the crunch, to get that *release*—and banging your head against a wall, or pretending to (depends on how much beer you've drunk), is the next higher level of aesthetic expression, particularly ecstatic when there's like a whole arena full of guys (and a few gals) doing approximately the same thing.

Mind you, this group and this record are probably "hard rock" rather than heavy metal, but fortunately you and I are not required to make or understand such distinctions. What does matter is, loud crunching joyous dumbness, preferably with a simple self-assertive message (and if possible sexual under- or overtones), is an essential unit of the pure rock coin. It is adolescent. It is eternal (my daughter, who wasn't born when the song came out, comes in to tell me how much she likes it). It feels good.

True dumb (innocent, enthusiastic crunch), if I can relax my self-importance and just get into it, makes me feel good. That's as opposed to contrived, manipulated dumb (check the list of top hits most weeks, most years), which always has an undertone of rip-off. I guess I'm saying I don't mind if you pull my strings ("she looked at me with those big brown eyes"), but don't do it cynically. Contrivance can be transformed by inspiration, as on "Drowning in the Sea of Love" or any of the great Motown recordings. We don't mind following, surrendering our egos to, the performance, as long as the songwriter and performer are themselves surrendering to and following Spirit.

Rock and roll, particularly the heavy metal/hard rock side of rock and roll, sometimes walks the (fine) line between anarchy and fascism. In this sense, dumb is dangerous. But smart is not the answer. Smart, when it denies the crude ancient powerful feelings that rule our hearts, when it refuses to acknowledge them or let them express themselves, is also dangerous. So what is the answer?

The answer is, take a risk. Scream, shout, stutter, pound the air with your fist, slam your body into the bodies next to yours and feel the thrill of abandon. Surrender to that adolescent illusion of immortality. It pulls us out of ourselves. "You ain't seen nothing yet!" Yeah. Let's go.

Take a risk and then take a further risk, the risk of being true to yourself. Maybe we can be smart about our dumbness, smell them coming when they pick up on our abandon and wrap the illusion of it in safe, gaudy, marketable, manipulable packages. Maybe. Maybe not.

Maybe I don't know the answer. But I do know good power chords when I hear them. Eternal vigilance is the price of freedom. I like this record.

*First release:* Mercury 76322, September 1974

# 69 Bob Marley and the Wailers

## *No Woman, No Cry*

Poverty, dignity, love, need, reassurance: this transcendently beautiful song and performance, recorded live in London by Jamaica's greatest ambassadors of reggae and of the spiritual/political/cultural (mystical) movement called Rasta, cuts clean to the heart of the matter in a few words, a few notes, a few moments of vibrant, soul-stirring clarity. This is one of the most comforting records I've ever pulled from a sleeve and fumbled onto a phonograph, even as it paradoxically makes me cry out in pain and awakeness as I sing along. Vocalist/preacher Marley takes on the classic (and sadly rare, in modern music, modern culture) masculine role of father, husband, elder brother, offering strength and hope to daughter/wife/sister in this the difficult but holy night where we endure, where we suffer, where we love and support one another and where we finally triumph. "Good friends we had, oh, good friends we lost/Along the way/In this great future you can't forget your past/So dry your tears I say." Don't worry baby. No woman, no cry.

No cry. The dignity of the song begins with its willingness to speak in its own language. If you have ears to hear, then (and only then) I am speaking to you. Song in general, song in its truest form, creates a willingness to hear by its attractive qualities, it captures, holds, and reshapes the attention of its listener, through its sincerity and integrity it opens us to new truth. Ancient truth also, for what truth is not ancient?, but new to us each day as we open our ears.

The rest of the song's dignity (by song I also mean performance, recording) lies in the calmness of the musical accompaniment, expressive of a wisdom and faith with roots that reach down through centuries and out across continents and oceans . . . and in the timbre of the singer's inimitable voice.

In songs coming out of the radio, singles rotating on a phonograph, we hear the voice of prophecy. The primary characteristic of prophecy is that it is a vehicle of revealed truth, belonging to the recipient and needing no validation from any outside authority. We hear, we recognize, we accept, we embrace, we know. And you are the humble radiant wild holy man whispering in our ears.

How appropriate, in this great future, that this voice can reach across cultures. And that when it reaches, it touches us in a place so local, so everyday, so modest and ennobled and human. "Said I remember, when we used to sit/In the government yard in Trenchtown . . . Then we would cook cornmeal porridge/Of which I'll share with you/My feet is my only carriage/So I've got to push on through." The Sermon on the Mount could hardly say it better. This is a song, a performance, about love.

And at its center (near the end, but at its center), the song blossoms out into holy cadenza, direct transmission of reassurance, an expression of faith that amounts to joyously shouldering the listener's, the family's, burden, something much more real and powerful (committed, honest) than talk. This passage is introduced (transitioned into) by the words "But while I'm gone I mean" and then Marley sings "Everything's gonna be all right" in harmony with Touter's organ and with the I-Threes (and the audience) singing and responding behind him, the same words over and over (eight times total) until we are permeated with them, and then triumphantly on to the exquisite chorus, "no woman, no cry," a moment of profound and subtle reconciliation of precious and ordinarily unspeakable truths.

Responsibility. There is a maturity in this song that is almost contradictory to the adolescent heartbeat that animates rock and roll, and yet it is properly rock and roll by its instrumentation, its structure, and its very ability to reach across contexts and confidently take center stage. Bob Marley a star, mon. A prophet. A great singer. A provider, survivor, believer. A visionary. A voice from the ether. A husband, a man. A person who gave us something that makes a difference in our struggle. He reminds us of the dignity of our lives.

*First release:* Island WIP 6244 (U.K.), August 1975

# 70 Bob Dylan

## *Hurricane (Part I)*

Wow. This is not one of the performances Bob Dylan is remembered for, but it should be. If Dylan is a Picasso (as Leonard Cohen insists), then "Hurricane" is his *Guernica*—a major work, masterwork, by a mature artist, that is a cry of anger and pain loudly calling attention to what is happening to real people here in this political world right now.

Footnotes aplenty. Rubin "Hurricane" Carter was a boxer convicted of murder who said he was innocent, he'd been framed; Dylan believed him and wrote this song with playwright Jacques Levy with the specific intention of publicizing the case and getting Carter out of jail. In the film *Renaldo & Clara* Dylan can be seen badgering the president of Columbia Records to release the song as a single as quickly as possible. Carter did get a lot of attention and a new trial, and was convicted again; this conviction was eventually overturned by a federal court in 1985, which said the decision had been based on "racism rather than reason." Carter was finally released in 1988 and the indictments against him were dropped—after he had spent twenty-one years in prison.

Technical footnote: The single consists of one (eight-and-a-half-minute) recording divided into two parts. "Part I" (first five verses) got most of the radio airplay, but if you own the single you can turn it over and hear the whole story, eleven verses, with hardly a pause for breath. Edited singles are a problem—I didn't include "Light My Fire" in this book because what was released as a single (center section edited out) is not a great record, even though the entire album track is what's usually played on the radio. Same situation with the Who's 1971 hit "Won't Get Fooled Again"—the album track is one of my all-time favorites, but the edited single doesn't begin to do it justice. In the case of "Hurricane," however, it's a great single even if you only listen to side one. The essence is there. Extraordinary songwriting. Phenomenal performance.

The single with its promise of immediate saturation airplay can be a powerful vehicle of political expression, but it has not often been used that way, perhaps largely because the airwaves are licensed by the central government in the U.S. and the U.K. both (with the exception of England's pirate radio era). Dylan earlier (1971) released an instant single called "George Jackson" about the death of an American political prisoner. The Who rush-released "The Last Time/Under My Thumb" in 1967, to protest the arrest on drug charges of members of the Rolling Stones. Crosby Stills Nash and Young put out "Ohio" ("How can you run when you know?") to protest the killings at Kent State in 1970. Peter Gabriel helped change the course of history with "Biko," his 1980 tribute to a martyred South African poet, and more recently Public Enemy and other rap groups have used the single and its offspring the rock video to make strong political statements. Pro-government singles also have turned up occasionally, such as Barry Sadler's 1966 smash "The Ballad of the Green Berets." In one notable case, Bruce Springsteen's "Born in the U.S.A.," sharply critical of American government practices, was widely misheard as a patriotic anthem and even embraced by the 1984 presidential candidates.

But enough footnoting. "Hurricane" is superb rock and roll: passionate, innovative, great melody, great lyrics, great beat, incredible phrasing, wonderful instrumentation (violin, congas), and a drive that doesn't quit, you can play it over and over and over, raising the volume every time until the walls shake. And they should. "In Paterson that's just the way things go/If you're black you might as well not show up on the street/Less you want to draw the heat." They goddamn well should.

*First release:* Columbia 3-10245, November 1975

# 71

## Patti Smith Group

# *Gloria*

Hark ye, the little lower layer. All visible objects, as Ahab told us, are but pasteboard masks. But in each event, each living act, some unknown but still reasoning thing puts forth its features from behind the unreasoning mask. If you follow me so far, I'm saying this record is about one's relationship with God, one's relationship with oneself, one's relationship with sex, and, not least, one's relationship with one's heritage: those monumental achievements that came before—like Them (or Van Morrison)'s "Gloria"—and pierced the veil of this reality the first time. Patti Smith is the herald of a new moment in rock and roll, third generation. She quotes Chuck Berry by quoting the Rolling Stones; lights candles to Hendrix and Jim Morrison; writes crazed brilliant anarchic poetry using "Land of 1000 Dances" as a lyrical and spiritual reference point.

She is not being cute. She is telling her truth. She is reaching for the thing behind the mask.

To do this, she puts on the mask. "Piss Factory," Patti's self-published 1974 single, was a great record; "Gloria," the single off her 1975 debut album *Horses,* is even better, a shout of pure joy and a shot of pure adrenaline—an unforgettable, irrevocable declaration of existence. Notice me, universe! Her song, which is not Van Morrison's "Gloria" but which contains and overlaps (or lapses into) it, begins with an invocation, an assertion, a blasphemous boast, and ends neatly with the same phrase repeated as final climax and benediction: (slow and deliberate) "Jesus died for somebody's sins, but not mine." This is a Catholic girl's proclamation of independence, in the breach because the very need to make it shows one is not as free as one might wish. A gambit, then. She steps forth proudly with impeccable attitude: "People say beware, but I don't care [sneer]/The words are just rules and regulations to me."

And then the story of a lesbian love affair. In the front part of the story, the singer is asserting her coolness ("I go to this here party and I just get bored") which is broken only by sexual desire ("I look out the window, see a sweet young thing . . . oh, she looks so good"), sexual fantasy that suddenly becomes real as the love object approaches ("here she comes!") and makes herself available for taking. The actual consummation takes place offstage on the single, a minute has been cut from the album version for reasons of propriety or, more probably, time; musically the track is stronger for the telescoping, but a key scene is lost (or made implicit)—"I look up at this big tower clock and say, 'Oh my God, it's midnight!' And my baby, she's walking through the door . . . she whispers to me . . ."

The song explodes into its centerpiece, Patti challenging Van Morrison and all the gods of her childhood, or rather challenging herself to strut up to them as an equal. With sublime support from her band (which has been with her each step of the way, making uncompromising, flawless rock and roll to match every mood and movement of her operetta), she sings "And her name is, and her name is . . ." and then bursts into the call-and-response, spell-it-out chorus of "Gloria," reaching for the sexiest and most powerful music she's heard in her whole life, measuring herself against the masters. And (breathless moment) she succeeds, and enters the ranks of the Immortals. The rest of the song reveals that this cocky seductress has fallen in love, other girls visit but "I didn't hear them, I didn't see/I let my eyes ride to the big tower clock/And I heard those bells talking in my heart, going 'DING DONG DING DONG DING DONG DING DONG DING DONG DING DONG DING DONG DING DONG/Remember the time, when you came in my room . . .' "

The quotes from the earlier song are brilliant: "so good," "and her name is," and the extraordinary build-up as lover approaches street, house, door, room. Most amazing of all though is what the daughter poet/storyteller/rock and roller does with the opening image of that song ("She comes around here just about midnight"): adds the bells, and discovers that sex and God and love are inseparable after all, strut though we may.

"If man will strike, strike through the mask! How can the prisoner reach outside except by thrusting through the wall? To me, the white whale is that wall, shoved near to me." "And her name is, and her name is, and her name is, and her name is . . ."

*First release:* Arista 0171, February 1976

# 72 The Sex Pistols

## *Anarchy in the U.K.*

What won't they think of next? It's 1976 (yeah history is stalking us again), only eight years since Mick Jagger complained that "sleepy London town is just no place for a street fighting man," and, uh, something has changed. It's no exaggeration to say this record is an act of aggression equivalent to throwing a bomb and/or spitting at, kicking, punching, and biting a stranger in a pub fight. It is certainly heavier than any heavy metal record I've ever heard. It's also as political as a musical performance can possibly be—it fully engages its listener in the issues it raises, whether listener wants to be engaged or not. It is as bold as Elvis in his brief shining moment. It doesn't just give the finger to the powers that be. It screams in their faces, demanding response (and dismissing that response before hearing it). It did this with enormous effect when it was first released—not a chart record in the United States, and it only got to #38 in the U.K, but it was *heard,* believe me—and still does it every time it finds its way to a phonograph. It does it with words, with sounds, with attitude as expressed through singing, and with attitude as expressed through guitar, bass, and drums screaming together. It is sarcastic, baiting, contemptuous, hate-filled. It speaks for that place in each of us that wants upheaval, revolution, honesty, at any cost. It is joyous. It is liberating. It is big noise.

Something was in the air, and when you play this record loud enough you can still smell the ozone. Rock and roll expresses a moment, which is why gestalt acts of creativity like this one are sometimes so successful, even though the various people involved may seem to be working at cross-purposes. Malcolm McLaren (manager) wanted fame, attention, self-importance, money. Johnny Rotten (born John Lydon) supposedly hated rock and roll but needed a job and couldn't resist the opportunity to have a go at everyone and anyone he might encounter. Matlock, Jones, and Cook were inexperienced wannabe rock musicians looking for fun, opportunity, a chance at self-expression. Punk was a feeling in the rooms where kids hung out, a rapidly intensifying (but unfocused and impotent) dissatisfaction with the world, specifically including comfortable old farts like the Stones, the Who, Led Zep, Bowie, persistent images of "youthful" rebellion who'd failed to die before getting so stinking old. The media and the music biz operators were all-powerful vain popinjays just begging to have their string pulled and their butts fucked. McLaren had an idea—possibly his only idea, but he believed in it and it was a timely one. He pushed the river in the direction it was going. So did Glen Matlock as he and his mates developed the remorseless, caterwauling sound of the Pistols. So did Johnny Rotten as he removed all restraints from the psychopathic side of his personality, Alex from *A Clockwork Orange* literally come to life, snarling and laughing into the microphone, "I am an antichrist." No dumbness. No posing. Simply the sincere desire to be your worst fears personified. "Now, don't worry." It's a very funny record. It's also unmistakably the real thing.

Creating something real is the most effective act of revolution, because it makes everything else look so stupid. When the big noise that rock and roll had been wanting to make for years or centuries suddenly broke through on this 45, it was like a bolt of lightning shattering the sky. Still is. The first fifty seconds are sheer ecstatic release: the thundering bass intro, the timing and energy of Rotten's opening words ("Right. Now!") and his amazing cackle, the breakneck tempo sustained through the first verse and into the start of the second, the rhyming of antichrist and anarchist, and the lovely summation of postindustrial youth's philosophical position, "Don't know what I want but I know how to get it!" Rotten's idiosyncratic phrasing, no word untwisted, is at the heart of the record's power, peaking in the final moments with the shouted mantra "Anarchist/Get pissed/Destroy." The last word extends itself until it unites with the last notes of the music, completing the cycle, a climax as devastating and exhilarating as the record's opening. Phew.

What won't they think of? Upsetting their own applecart. But don't worry. Just stand there long enough, and some punk will be glad to come along and do it for you.

*First release:* EMI 2566 (U.K.), November 1976

# 73 Television

## *Marquee Moon*

Elsewhere. Let me take you away from this. A good poem, a good record, pulls you up by the roots in its first sweep of words, sounds, images, and you let go oh so naturally and easily and allow yourself to be transported. In music we travel. Where? Here. Place that sounds like this. Oh. I like it. Is there some other way to get here? No, man, only this record . . .

Here is elsewhere. And the feel of the place is so much more important than understanding the story the guy is telling. The fact that he's telling a story, that's what comes across. And um, the way the bones in his face (face reflected by voice) seem to glow in the urban moonlight. Urban junkyard by moonlight. And this strange guy is sitting on an engine block or something, and he's telling a story. Weaving a yarn. Laconically, taking his time. And you're just sitting here hypnotized by the sound of his two-guitar voice.

And the beat. The guitars and the beat. Same old elements. Utterly new combinations. Fresh and familiar. I've never been here before. But I like it. It stirs up such *feelings*—

It's amazing that a record could be so self-consciously mysterious, so overtly romantic, and still achieve true mystery. I mean, these chords have been lying around forever, how come no one else—since, say, Country Joe & the Fish on their great "Section 43" EP in 1966—has showcased them? Records like this (and there is no other record quite like this, that's part of the point) are rock and roll rediscovered, again and again, bold eccentric excursions that return to the mainline in order to rediscover the primal territory that the best music lives in, invades, expresses, illuminates. Rediscover and make new. Because it is new. "Marquee Moon" is as eccentric and original and seminal as Jimi Hendrix or the Velvet Underground. It is a reclaiming—as those artists' works were, in the sense that all our creations, perhaps, have their roots in our childhood experiences, original mystery—of sacred ground.

The song comes over us in waves. Three waves, or sets of waves, tense at the start with staccato guitar dialog, building through the verse which is a kind of self-contained call and response ("I was listening" "Listening to the rain" "I was hearing" "Hearing something else"), into the chorus which is ecstatic, climactic, and a perfect example of how much more we hear sometimes when we can't hear the lyrics (the words printed on the album sleeve are so much less than what his voice communicates), yodeling in tongues, wave cresting and breaking as the words " 'neath the Marquee Moon" float free from the chaos. The structure is very deliberate: first wave is followed by the words "Just waiting"; second time, "hesitating"; third and last time, "I ain't waiting!" On the single the instrumental outburst that follows fades after a minute or so (the other four minutes of the jam and brief vocal reprise are on the B-side of the seven-inch; there was also a twelve-inch disc with the whole ten minutes on one side). Until now I hadn't heard the song as a single (it was a modest hit—#30—in the U.K.). I like it tremendously, not that one version or the other is "better" but that this early fade invites that special relationship we have with a single, listen over and over, dive into those waves, deeper and deeper each time, lost in ecstasy and new territory and wonder. Repetition is a great tool for spiritual awakening. Lean into the mystery. Immerse yourself. Play it again.

Ticket to elsewhere. The formula is simple. You hear/feel this sound in your head. It's just out of reach—and clear as a vision. You learn instrument, join band, battle egos in band and out, till your crazy ego triumphs over or with the others and screams/sings its song to the world. Going for the sound. Everything for the sound. Because when you get the sound, the place follows. The story follows. The wave breaks, and billows. The guitars speak the truth about where we are. Listen . . .

*First release:* Elektra K 12252 (U.K.), March 1977

# 74

## James Taylor

# *Handy Man*

Another holy record. It touches every part of me. I know there's a belief that people who like the Sex Pistols couldn't possibly like James Taylor, and vice versa, but of course it's not true. Outside of our little boxes, where we've been put either by others who need focused market data, or by ourselves who need the security of identity and belonging, outside these boxes I say we recognize only what speaks to our hearts, and the form in which it speaks or the flag it flies make no difference whatsoever once true contact has been made. The greatness of the single, in its era, was its ability to reach out across the airwaves beyond preconceptions and marketing categories, not normally (safe "marketable" garbage being the norm for top 40 radio almost always, of course) but exceptionally, now and then, and those glorious exceptions are what matter. Are what shape us. Are what raise us up to be powerful, awakened beings, unembarrassed by either the violent passion of "Anarchy in the U.K." or the sweet vulnerability of "Handy Man." We recognize power objects. When they speak to us, we approach them, listen more closely. When they go on speaking, we embrace them, become them. This is the process. This is how we grow beyond our boxes. This is how we find who we're able to be.

The subject of "Handy Man" is sexual healing. That was not the subject of the original version, or if it was I didn't get it—true I was twelve years old, but I don't think that was the problem. Jimmy Jones's record was annoying, boastful, glib. James Taylor's version is gently confident, seductive in the very best sense of the word, pulling us gently and irresistibly into its world of reassurance and restoration of what's been lost. Such an amazing arrangement. Every note in place (new place, waited-for place, never-before-arrived-at place). Every hook so delicious I open my fish-mouth wide and bite hard. "Come-a come-a come-a come-a come come (come)." Dream language.

Heaven rock. And running through this lighter-than-air, infinitely penetrating mixture of foreground voice, back voices, guitar, bass and drums, is the unchanging, unshakable message: you can be healed. I can do it. I'm the one. I'm your handy man.

Voice from the radio like the voice of Heaven, or one of Heaven's angels. Angels don't boast. They simply whisper the news.

And then the further level is that this is a man singing, after all, and what he's offering is himself, and what he's singing about is sex. We listen as women who'd like to be visited by the handy man. We listen as men who'd like to have his job.

We listen as persons being courted by another person.

And what we hear is so sweet. The opening guitar notes are sweet (slow riff, but riff nonetheless, irresistible as moonlight). The tempo is sweet. The strings are sweet, and tasteful. Taylor's tone of voice is impeccable throughout. The ending is exquisite ("Yeah, yeah yeah"). Peter Asher (producer) and Taylor and whoever else made this arrangement used all their conscious skill and experience and cleverness, sure, but they also tapped into something. And it's that something that comes through, that lets me listen ten times, twenty times, over and over and still I'm pulled in, still something in me is spoken to and I feel the power of my response.

I believe in sexual healing, and so I believe in the shaman-casanova this song postulates and creates. I don't believe he's a man, or a woman, or any one person. But he or she works through individual persons. Not often. But sometimes. And when it happens—when it happens to you—when it happens through you—you know what miracles are.

And the sound of what that feels like has been captured in the grooves of this record.

*First release:* Columbia 10557, May 1977

# 75 Jonathan Richman and the Modern Lovers

## *Roadrunner*

Another anomaly (Jonathan wouldn't have it any other way). The single I've selected here was released in the U.K. in 1977; however the A-side was originally recorded, and released as a single in the U.S., in 1975. The U.K. B-side—same song, same title, same lead singer—was recorded in 1971 (part of the legendary Modern Lovers demo tapes, produced by John Cale, unreleased until 1976). The disc gets placed here with the 1977 entries because both versions are magnificent, and rather than choose between them I offer this two-sided, one-song single, which made it to #11 on the British charts. (Both versions also received considerable airplay in the U.S. thanks to college radio stations.)

But enough small talk. Start the music. Jonathan Richman's "Roadrunner" is one of the most quoted rock and roll songs of all time—that's musical quotes, mostly—and is itself, as Mojo Nixon and Skid Roper demonstrated in their 1985 tour de force "Jesus at McDonald's," a brilliant (musical) restatement of the Velvet Underground's masterpiece, "Sister Ray." This riff may or may not be the heart of rock and roll (we can fight about that later), but it's certainly the heart of *something.* Won't quit. Keeps turning up. Can't get it out of our minds. That's 'cause it's in our blood. Could in fact be the sound of the human circulatory system hustling to keep up with the particular stimuli of our epoch, the "modern world" Jonathan refers to again and again in the course of this (doubly) epic performance.

Rock and roll has been self-referential since "Rock Around the Clock" or earlier, but still it's arguable that "Roadrunner" is the all-time greatest (most primal) expression of the inexpressible SIGNIFICANCE of driving around in a car late at night listening to the radio, that means music, A.M., the place where (once upon a time) the hits were played. Rock and roll.

"I say roadrunner once, roadrunner twice/We're in love with this feeling now, and we'll be out all night." Resume riff. 50,000 watts of power. Oh yeah.

Essence of garage band. Precursor of punk. Natural descendant of "Wake Up, Little Suzie" and "Magic Bus": acoustic hard rock. Side B is a little "heavier" and features a great Question-Mark-and-the-Mysterians organ performance by Jerry Harrison (Farfisa?). Side A offers, in its climactic movement, some of the most amazing scat singing ever heard on a rock and roll record: "I feel alone in the cold and neon (*radio on*)/I feel alive, I feel alone, I feel alive, I feel a rockin' modern love (*radio on*)/I feel a rockin' modern live, I feel a (*radio on*) rockin' modern neon modern sound modern Boston town (*radio on*)/A modern sound modern neon modern miles around (*radio on*)/I say uh roadrunner once red roadrunner twice, hit road now (*radio on*) hold on very nice, roadrunner going, I'm go home now, yes (*radio on*) make me go home/Oh yes roadrunner go home, here we go/We're gonna drive him home you guys . . ." Both versions start "1, 2, 3, 4, 5, 6, roadrunner, roadrunner." Both versions end with great simple orgasmic rhythmic conclusiveness, and the shouted words, "Bye bye!"

Start the music. You could be scared off, consecutively, by the noisiness of "Anarchy," the off-tune guitars in "Marquee Moon," the slick quietness of "Handy Man," and now the monstrously flat vocals in "Roadrunner." And you might be missing precisely what it is that makes each song itself—and all of them, arguably, great rock and roll. Rock and roll is idiosyncratic. *Greatness* is idiosyncratic. "Roadrunner" is a song about being your own person, and being supported in this by the universe ("radio on" is the Logos, Godhood alive and kicking), and loving the world exuberantly as a result. The drums on this record are as ticky-tack gorgeous as on Chuck Berry's "Memphis." And the *feeling* of a group playing and singing together is as palpable as on, say, the earliest Beatles records. The future of rock and roll is here too, of course. The whole damn thing caught in one timeless snapshot. "I'm in love with the modern world/Massachusetts when it's late at night/And the neon when it's cold outside . . .

"You see, I have the radio on."

*First release:* Beserkley BZZ 1 (U.K.), June 1977

# 76 The Sex Pistols

## *Holidays in the Sun*

More noise. And so delicious. I can't think of a record I'd rather clear a room with. "I don't understand this bit at all." Yes, well. What we have here is a political statement that goes light years beyond the basic "fuck you!" of "Anarchy in the U.K." and "God Save the Queen" and "Pretty Vacant," the other three Sex Pistols singles ("Holidays" was their fourth and last, not counting gobs of scraped-together "product" released after the group's demise). Standing up in bold opposition to the powers that be ("We're so pretty, oh so pretty . . . *vacant;* and we don't care!") is such a fundamental expression of political awakening that in a way it's hard to conceive of anything else to say that's politically relevant (except of course the counterpart, defending the status quo, not a familiar stance for rock and rollers but stay tuned for the next entry). There *is* something else, however, and "Holidays" says it as loud and "clear" as it's ever been articulated: the emperor has no clothes. That's not good or bad in and of itself (unless you have a strong position about nudism); what's significant about it is the calling attention to a central reality that consensus perception ignores, denies, or cannot see. "I don't understand this bit at all." *That*'s meaningful information. Beyond "fuck you!," and the endless "You're wrong but I'm right" battles that always result in "meet the new boss, same as the old boss," lies the possibility of actually expanding our collective awareness and coming to grips with a little more of what is. And this starts by noticing the holes in our happy consensus. The mysteries. 1977. The Berlin Wall. WHAT THE FUCK DOES IT MEAN?

Musically this is an extremely muscular record, riff fat enough to knock down walls with, perfectly focused angry vocals, guitars that make you fantasize your own fingers doing the slashing, take that! Exhausting, exhilarating. It satisfies. Lyrically—well, the words are hard to catch, but they come through after a while, and if you have an original copy it comes in one of my all-time-favorite picture sleeves, cute family-on-holidays cartoons (on the front) with balloon dialogue drawn from the lyrics. I.e., boy and girl playing in the sand, she's saying "I don't want a holiday in the sun. I wanna go to the new Belsen," and he's saying, "I wanna see some history cos I got a reasonable economy." Grinning pseudo-hip young couple in front of handsome Teutonic architecture, he saying, "A cheap holiday in other people's misery" (the muffled opening words of the record, how's that for bitterly sarcastic social commentary that somehow goes beyond simple moralizing?).

The point is, the person singing the song has the remarkable idea of going (to the Continent) to see some "history" that is present rather than past, questions his own reasons for doing so each step of the way, but anyway inexorably finds himself at the base of this inexplicable monolith separating "us" from "them" and somehow rising up out of the subconscious to dwarf and mock everyday perceptions of "Europe" and "the modern world" and "what's going on." He finds himself perplexed, obsessed, and musically as well as lyrically we hear and feel him throwing himself against the Wall, wanting to go over it, under it, squirming in his discomfort and compulsion and fear, a fear most of all of whatever may be on the "other" side if he actually gets there.

The music says it all: a song about throwing yourself down the stairs. You don't have to understand a word of it, and you'll still get the feeling. Nihilism of the most dangerous kind—the kind that leads to lonely, terrifying awakeness rather than blissed-out self-destruction. "Now I've got a reason to be waiting: The Berlin Wall." Now and then there's a painting, a poem, a record that cuts through the traps, the endless pseudo-profound cycles of ordinary consciousness. Something that clears the mental room. An inspired noise, a wall-smasher. A big bold arrow pointing to, rubbing our noses in, the mysteries we cheerfully pretend we understand.

"Holidays in the Sun" is that sort of record. It has the stink, and the roar, of genius.

*First release:* Virgin VS 191 (U.K.), October 1977

# 77

## Queen

# *We Will Rock You/ We Are the Champions*

The strangest thing about a compact disc is that it only has one side. There's nothing underneath. Cassette singles, on the other hand, are two-sided devices pretending to be one-sided, since side B is normally an exact duplicate of side A. No top, no bottom. (Endless loops, especially if you have auto reverse.) The 45, however, subject of this book even though it starts with a 78 and ends with a cassette/CD ("no U.S. vinyl"), is inherently two-sided, with the further delightful twist that the up-side is public like a face (you can hear it on the radio) and the down-side is private like the thoughts in your head, only for the buyer, only for those curious enough, adventurous enough, to turn the record over. Take a walk on the B-side.

"We Will Rock You/We Are the Champions" is a two-sided single (meaning both sides were hits). More than that, it is the only single I know that fully takes advantage of the two-sidedness of the medium—the only single in which the interaction between the two recordings is at the core of what the group is consciously communicating. (An example of a semi- or unconscious juxtaposition is "Penny Lane"/"Strawberry Fields Forever," two songs about places, in which each of the Beatles' two assumed personas—the John-head and the Paul-head—goes for baroque separately and simultaneously, each in a manner intended to dazzle the universe with just how much can be squeezed onto one side of a 45-rpm record.)

The two sides of Queen's single were also the first two tracks of an album, and in the U.S. many radio stations played the two together as though they were one track ("We Will Rock You" first, of course). Again, I cannot think of another instance in which a hit song was actually two songs played one after the other (as opposed to two songs medleyed into one, like

"Aquarius/Let the Sunshine In"). The point is, anyway, that even the deejays got the point: the single as a whole is a response to the punks by an established rock band (no one but Queen had the balls to do this), with one song, "We Will Rock You," written by guitarist Brian May, expressing the (romantic/pathetic) punk side of themselves and of us all, and the other song, "We Are the Champions," written by vocalist Freddie Mercury, expressing the rock star side. Both songs, as their titles clearly state, are "fuck you!" anthems, one written from the viewpoint of the grimy streets and the other (a perspective rarely acknowledged openly in rock and roll, although it's certainly where most name rock and rollers do their observing from) the luxury suites.

It's wonderful. "We Will Rock You," which is a capella with handclap/foot-stomp accompaniment until the guitar solo in the final seconds, vibrates with crude angry youthful energy full of pride and bluster (and impotence and self-loathing just under the surface), smart subtle lyrics just made to be chanted (". . . gonna take on the world someday/You got blood on your face, you big disgrace/Waving your banner all over the place")—in the class structure of rock and roll this song speaks for the young turks, the nobodies, the contenders. And even as the verses acknowledge the dead-end destinies that the poor are largely condemned to, the guitar coda soars free and speaks of the power of the individual human spirit to somehow spit in the eye of Fate and break out of this prison.

Other side, next song, the boy who broke free is now the prince in the tower. And in this version (not the self-pity of Pete Townshend in the '70's nor the self-exploitation of Mick Jagger), he's proud of having fought his way to the top and is ready to fight (creatively, commercially, name your poison) to maintain his position: "You've brought me fame and fortune and everything that goes with it, I thank you all/But it's been no bed of roses, no pleasure cruise/I consider it a challenge before the whole human race and I ain't gonna lose!" This is done with humor (music building from sensitive art-rock to thundering heavy metal, Moody Blues meet Led Zep, pastiche history of an era) and sincerity: you think it looks easy, kid, come up here and try it some time.

Class struggle. Haves vs. have-nots. Where does rock and roll stand? Would you like to think of us as (and identify yourselves with) the lads arriving in the limo, or the ruffians gathering outside to push it over? No need to decide yet. Flip the record. And again. And one more time . . .

*First release:* EMI 2708 (U.K.), October 1977

# 78 The Only Ones

## *Another Girl, Another Planet*

This is my fantasy, and the weird thing is that it doesn't come true more often: someone looks at my list of best singles and says, "Hey, what about—?", and it's something I've never heard of, and I listen to it and right away I love it, wow, it fills an emptiness I didn't even know was there, life is worthwhile and the world is a better place.

So here's to the guy with the Brooklyn accent in a pub in Manchester in 1990, who not only told me about this song but pulled a CD-player and an assortment of favorite CD's out of his travel bag and initiated me on the spot. The Only Ones can't be called one-hit wonders because "Another Girl, Another Planet" didn't make the charts in the U.S. or their native U.K., even though it's the sort of single which if you heard it out of the blue you'd call the radio station right away to get the name of the artist, and you wouldn't be surprised to find it #1 in the world six weeks later. Yeah, well. Sometimes lightning strikes, and sometimes it misses.

But oh what a perfect record. A great single starts with the opening notes, they should have a rhythm in them, something distinctive and irresistible, arouses you and changes your mood the instant it hits your eardrums, sets your whole being in motion. And then when the voice finally comes in it's just who you wanted to hear from: the *sound* of the voice, reflection of inner self, sweet imaginary friend from early childhood, and the words so charming and unsettling, "I always flirt with death, I'll get killed but I don't care about it," slurred, that's not exactly what he says, this is the sort of record that always leaves space for ambiguity, and best of all keeps going, "I think I'm on another world with you, with you," keeps you going, keeps me going, joyous heartbeat of the unseen, constantly felt universe.

"Space travel's in my blood, there is nothing I can do about it." Charming. And more. It connects.

From out of nowhere. It connects.

This is it, the miracle of the single, this is what it's about. This record isn't linear. It cuts across something. Cuts to the quick. Cuts through. Those voices. Always known them. Never heard them before. You know what I'm talking about. The airwaves. The ether. The melody. We are connected. This is the evidence. "Another girl is holding you now." Wait, that changes the whole meaning of the song. But not really. Speaking in tongues. Holy babble (content-rich, nonlinear, irresistible distinctive rhythm). Connection. How we get in touch with ourselves.

How does it do what it does? Silly question, but I have an answer so I'll share it: sincerity and inspiration. The two feed each other, and are rarer than we think. So much stuff can get in the way. But occasionally it all comes together at the right moment and we get a miracle.

How many more are hiding out there somewhere? Enough to last a lifetime. That's not my fantasy. It's my basic article of faith. If I can just keep my heart and ears open— ("with you, with you . . .")

*First release:* CBS 6228 (U.K.), April 1978

# 79

## Talking Heads

# *Take Me to the River*

Every great performance has the ghosts of past performances inside it. In this case our screams (you're not listening to this record right if you don't find yourself screaming along with the chorus) are no doubt requesting transportation to that greatest of American waterways, drainer of the heartlands, the Mississippi, because although David Byrne and Talking Heads may have laid down this deep groove in some ofay New York City recording studio, the song and performance they're emulating is by Syl Johnson and Willie Mitchell out of Al Green and Teenie Hodges out of Little Junior Parker, that is to say, MEMPHIS MEMPHIS MEMPHIS (now I'm screaming), the great portal of American music, delta on one side and southside Chicago on the other, south and north, country and city, and Memphis in between (in the meantime, as John Hiatt has it) . . . "Take Me to the River" was first recorded by Al Green in 1974, one of the climaxes of his live act but it didn't catch on as a single until Willie Mitchell, who produced Al's version and just about everything else Hi put out in the early '70's, recorded Syl Johnson's version, which was a top 10 r&b hit in 1975. It's a weird song, lyrically—the singer seems to be referring obliquely to an affair with a sixteen-year-old girl, asking for redemption, spiritual cleansing, and an opportunity to go on with the relationship. "I haven't seen how to help you yet . . . I want to know, won't you tell me, I'd love to stay . . ." Talking Heads take hold of the song and put the emphasis almost entirely on the spiritual side of things, which they can do precisely because baptism is an exotic concept to them and their audience, unlikely to be taken literally and therefore able to pull forth all sorts of unspoken feelings and images. David Byrne, as is his wont, swallows the lyrics ("I haven't seen worst of it yet . . . I want to know, can you tell me? I uh to ayyyyyyy . . ."), focusing the entire energy of the performance on the title phrase and its echo ("take me to the river, drop me in the water"), repeated and reshuffled ("drop me in the river, push me in the water") in a hypnotic chant. As for Junior Parker, Al Green refers to him overtly in a spoken introduction to his recorded version, "Like to dedicate this song to Little Junior Parker, a cousin of mine, he's gone on but we'd like to kind of carry on in his name." This bit of talking actually gets in the way of Al's record, but it's important because Talking Heads are doing the same thing just by recording a "cover" version, the *I Ching* says "the way to study the past is not to confine oneself to mere knowledge of history but, through application of this knowledge, to give actuality to the past," and this process is a lot more central to rock and roll than you might think. We sing about God and sex. And always, at the same time, we sing about music—expressing what we've learned from music—expressing what we've learned from music about God and sex. The past is the river, as Heraclitus or somebody told us (present and future also), and the music—

—takes us there and pushes us in.

"I don't know why I love you like I do." Now it starts to make sense. "All the changes you put me through." (Turn up the volume.) "I want to know, can you *tell me . . . ?"* All right, I feel it, I'm ready to scream now (I like this record, makes me bang my hands together on the off-beat)—

All three versions are wonderful. This one's on the list because it's most universal, it includes (and, happily, leads us to) the others, Chris Frantz and Tina Weymouth aren't quite the Hi rhythm section but they give actuality to that rhythm section in a way that is sometimes even more exciting than the real thing. It's like, they become the river. Like I scream along with their lead singer, they scream (through their instruments) along with all that Memphis music in their heads. And hearts. Washing me down. Washing me—

A song about ghosts. How we throw ourselves in the river. How we—maybe we never even heard Junior Parker, doesn't matter—how we carry on in his name.

*First release:* Sire 1032, November 1978

# 80 Dire Straits

## *Sultans of Swing*

My relationship with music is more important to me than my relationship with rock and roll. This goes without saying (I think), yet even today how few of us will automatically put planet ahead of nation. Old values die hard. And that's what this song is about. Music, yes; one of the truly great song-poems that is overtly about the love of music (listening to it and performing it, both). But more than that. This is a song about values.

How then shall we live? We answer this question at every moment, yet we ask it far too seldom. In this amazing debut single, singer/guitarist Mark Knopfler tells a story, a story in which one thing happens: the protagonist ("you") gets caught by the "sound of the rhythm" from a local jazz club while walking at night in the rain; he goes inside and stays till the band retires for the evening. That's all. Boy hears music; music gets boy (or girl, as the case may be).

Values. "Sound of the rhythm you stop and you hold everything." The world stops, makes way, for something (that you recognize as) more important. You have just responded to spirit, and let go of habit. You have opened yourself to something. You have been called by, responded to, and entered a higher realm.

Meanwhile on stage, the Sultans are expressing *their* values. The storyteller makes it clear that there aren't many people in the club, that the gig doesn't pay well, that the members of the younger generation present are not impressed—in short, that this band has no hope whatsoever of "making it big" or even making it at all in financial terms. They're here because they live for this ("saving it up for Friday night"). It is not a stepping-stone to someplace else. It is, take it or leave it, the meaning of their lives, and much of the record's greatness is the tremendous respect it evokes in every listener for these persons (whether they happen to be great musicians or not) and the choices they've made.

The ways they've chosen to live.

Music is our meeting place. (I'm speaking now of performer and listener.) What else, apart from sex, is so consistently intimate? "Sultans of Swing" is a song about falling in love; it celebrates its own listener (shows us how strongly and easily we identify with the protagonist), even though, paradoxically, the music it storytells about and the music it makes are very different animals. Or are they? The further triumph of the performance, arguably, is that it reveals the existence of the one very different music (Dixieland jazz) inside the other (contemporary pop/rock and roll). "But the horns they blowing that sound." This line sums up both the listener's and the performers' story with exquisite clarity and understatement, and as it's sung we hear those horns. Knopfler plays electric guitar over a rock and roll rhythm section, and we feel horns, especially in the climactic burst of soloing that ends the song and the story. Magic.

Our meeting place. Music's greatest value may be its power to remind us of our values, of what's truly important. Taking the bull by the horns, is this record, which is certainly beautifully realized and full of spirit, and which has probably sold four or five million copies at least around the world, more important in some way than one night's show by a good local band of whatever musical persuasion? No. I don't think so. It can't be. Experience is not hierarchical or numerical. Experience happens to each of us, one person at a time, one moment at a time.

The key word is "important." How do we know what this word means? We can't find out from a dictionary. But we can find out (we can be reminded) by direct experience: "coming in out of the rain to hear the jazz go down."

Sweet, surprising gift, this record. Out of nowhere. Brilliant hook (the title phrase, a sort of self-mockery combined with self-affirmation), which Knopfler arrogantly and cleverly makes us wait three minutes for, it only comes twice in the almost six minutes of the song, and such a gentle and fulfilling release when it does come: "We are the Sultans, we are the Sultans of Swing."

Music gets boy. And girl. And brings us home.

*First release:* Warner 8736, January 1979

# 81

Anita Ward

## *Ring My Bell*

"You can ring my bell, anytime, anywhere . . ." What an amazing promise this is! My phonograph just reminded me of how easily we take its miracle (any miracle) for granted—reminded me by breaking down in the middle of the song, forgetting momentarily how it knows what speed to rotate at. Needless to say I hadn't the slightest idea how to restore the lost information. But I monkeyed around for a few moments, and the song came back, right speed right pitch all those good things, and me a lot humbler, less cocky, more aware I might lose this treasure (this song playing over and over and over as I bliss out in ecstasy) any breathing moment. I am powerless.

Start over. "You can ring my bell, anytime, anywhere." What if that were true? My first response is a great rush of physical pleasure, happiness, well-being, but that's because I naturally hear her words as being spoken (sung) to me and me alone. How glorious to be so welcomed, reassured, wanted, accepted. How thrilling to hear her yes, to be the one.

But wait. What if she says the same thing to someone else? Now my feelings are all turned upside down, inside out, ass backward. Comfort turns to rage. That's not what this song is about, don't get me wrong, but just possibly it explains why some of my friends look down the list and single this song out as one of the few they strongly object to. A disco smash. It offends them. We're talking angels and whores here, that subtle distinction that brings madness to so many men's minds (and women's too, in a slightly different way), the distinction between the pure spirit who makes her blessing available only and always to one person, to me, and that impure being whose very sin is her availability, her cheapening of the holy through her indiscriminate generosity. Whore of Babylon. Desecrator of the temple. Some people hate disco categorically, even as they sanctify Motown or Chuck Berry or the Beatles or other artworks created for specifically commercial purposes. Why is that? Well, for some historical reason or other (no need for us to go back and try to find the particular circumstance), they associate it with a cheapening of the Goddess (for someone else it might be Elvis doing ballads), they equate disco with a loss of something magical, something private, something experienced as exclusive, angelic, utterly personal and holy and reassuring. A very slight shift, you see, between hearing her speaking just to you (or hey, hearing me speaking just to you, there's no one else reading this book right now is there?) and between perceiving her as some record in a jukebox warbling her "anytime, anywhere" to absolutely anyone who'll drop a quarter in the slot.

What I mean is, people feel manipulated by disco. Okay, all right. But that's exactly the same feeling that people from some other historical context (grew up with Louie Armstrong, or Frank Sinatra and Bing Crosby) get when confronted by (any kind of) rock and roll. Impurification of the holy (Song, Music). Cheap manipulation of what should be sacred. Get thee behind me, Satan.

Relax already. Start over, again. This is an exquisite record. Maybe it is one of the first big hits to use a synthesized drum, which yeah is against my personal religion no question about it, but why should I allow ideas or information to get in the way of true love and beauty (especially given that none of us gets out of here alive and my phonograph could break down again at any moment)? Listen. Listen to the impossibly seductive innocent openness and knowingness of Anita Ward's voice on this her first and only hit record (judging from the flip, she deserved a longer career). Listen to the extraordinary track created by producer Frederick Knight, perfectly tuned (every rhythmic moment, every percussive emphasis, every rise and fall in that inaudible and everpresent bass line) not only to the vocal but to the listener's response to the vocal, nanosecond to nanosecond, hey I know the track was recorded first but it doesn't matter, it all works backward, first my response (and oh, all those other people's) as they hear this #1 record from their car radio, then singer singing in such a way as to get that response, then Fred Knight inventing and playing and scoring and programming exactly the only music hot enough and regular enough and in synch enough with these words, this mood, this moment, to exalt that vocal. Backward further to the elements that brought together singer, producer, song, record label opportunity and so forth. No space left to tell you why I love this record so much. It's too private anyway. Frankly, I don't want to share it. Go away, and take all your friends with you. Anita and I just want to be alone together.

*First release:* Juana 3422, April 1979

# 82 Lipps, Inc.

## *Funkytown*

Dance is silly. Don't you forget it. It's not the only component of dance, of course, but it's one of the more important ones, often overlooked by "serious" commentators. The silliness of dance, whether it's the mashed potatoes or an old-fashioned square dance or rave or even ballroom, is what allows us as participants to get past inhibitions and self-consciousness into the liberation of actual movement. "Don't worry about making a fool of yourself," the other dancers say with their bodies, "we're *all* making fools of ourselves." Tonight, the fool in you and the fool in me are invited to come out and play. Get down. Get funky. Start foolin' around. All right!

"Funkytown" is, according to my favorite dancer, a "delightfully synthetic" record, "like knowing it's polyester, and not giving a damn" (thanks, Donna). What makes it delightful, ironically, is its humanness: its humor, its playfulness, the obvious, unselfconscious joy of creation that comes through at every moment. Big, bold colors. Circus music, carousel music. Simple enough and bright enough to bring a smile to the face of any four-year-old, and a bounce to his or her little body. Rhythm and sound. A multi-instrumentalist, like Steven Greenberg who wrote and produced this record and probably played all the instruments (if indeed there are any instruments here other than the synthesizer), is in a sense a person who hears rhythms and harmonies and counterpoints and all manner of musical interactions inside himself, a conductor who carries around with him his own orchestra, multiple personalities pushing and pulling and shouting for attention somehow brought together into a unified front, a performance, in which all these forces are in radiant dynamic relation to each other, making music, making silliness, making us smile and wiggle and dance. Transporting us, as requested, to that place of Otherness:

Won't you take me to

Funkytown?

Oh yes. Lay out the map now. Metronomic bass riff first (but with an edge, an energy, not hypnotic but kinetic), and now the Farfisa-like organ riff comes in (grandson of steam calliope), repeated twice, and if you don't know how much you like just hearing it by itself on top of the bass riff you'll find out two-thirds of the way through the record when the clean riff returns and you get an experience of pure hook, *this* is what I was waiting for, oops gone again . . . Third piece in the puzzle is female voice through vocoder, "Gotta make a move to a town that's right for me," unearthly and marvelous, bass riff under and organ riff after, another vocoder line and then pow! the woman bursts free of the machine and we hear clear human voice shouting, "Well I talk about it talk about it talk about it talk about it!", repeated with variation and mini-climax: "Talk about talk about talk about *moving!"* Insistent riff continues, of course, and (inspired moment) words now add themselves to the first section of the organ part: "Gotta move on." These four syllables merge with the ten-beat riff so that we hear in our minds something like, "gotta move on, (beat), I gotta move on," and for the rest of the record organ will sing these words to us whether accompanied by (sort of) human voice or not. Next the basic bass riff is transformed into a descending bass run which bottoms out into a wonderfully satisfying percussive scratching, then bass back up into (another hook) the introduction of guitar riff, which is married always to singer crying "Won't you take me to . . . Funkytown?", guitar punctuation before and after title word.

And that's hardly the end—after guitar/voice section there's the guitar/"strings" section, and the drums/horns section, more guitar/voice and then back to the beginning, it sounds exhausting but it's actually neat as a pin and, in the right mood (say two out of every three times you hear it), light as a feather.

And you'd think the guy who could invent and record this would have us by the gonads, knows exactly how and where and when to make us jump, but no, far as I know he never got another hit.

Which is to say, silliness ain't as simple as it appears. You can follow the map but you can't program in the magic. There is no specific road to Otherness (except maybe *find a riff and ride it*). "Won't you take me to . . . ?"

*First release:* Casablanca 2233, March 1980

# 83 Joy Division

## *Love Will Tear Us Apart*

Accentuate the negative. Why not? It's as much a part of the truth as the positive, some days quite more so, and the truth will set us free, won't it? Maybe, maybe not. Probably not. Accentuate the negative. This record bends over backward not to offer any hope, and I don't want to break the spell. The proper response to a great single, regardless of the mood it speaks to, is to let yourself be drawn in deeper and deeper. Misery loves company. Come closer, old buddy. We're going to celebrate you now. This record is the companion you've been looking for.

Hurts so good. Some kinds of pain are dramatic, but that won't do for depression. Lack of affect, not wailing and moaning, is the flag of resignation. I belong to the blank generation. Before punk, after punk, there's a pain of separateness that can't long be cured by attitude or by illusion of community. Tell the truth about it—musically and rhythmically as well as lyrically—that's all you can do. Tell it well enough and a kind of upside-down joy emerges, the thrill of self-expression. Joy with a kick in it, that great title melodic hook. The kick being the bad news the words convey. You're cute when you're despairing. Take that, Captain and Tennille (this being the answer song to their big hit "Love, Love Will Keep Us Together"). Ah, sweet release of sharing, wallowing in, these persistent feelings of no release.

I love the simple ecstatic aggression of the intro. Like "Pinball Wizard" but more modest, grittier, somehow a smidgeon closer to my Platonic ideal of the opening of a rock and roll record. That is to say, very close indeed. How come I like this mechanical drum sound so much? Because the issue is not mechanics. It's *sound.* There's a rightness here. I can't describe it; I can hear it. I can feel it. Drums every bit as expressive as the no-affect vocals, and the interplay between the two is astonishing, the beat pulls the words back, endlessly, catching the listener in a tidal backwash that becomes a swirling maelstrom when the synth joins in, adding melody and moodiness and an insistent misdirection. Occasional guitar bursts complete the picture, plus the (synthesized?) ringing guitars that enter when vocals depart, charmingly teasing out the instrumental fade with flashes of Byrds ("Bells of Rhymney") and Spector ("Then He Kissed Me") mixed into the preindustrial drone.

Sound. The most apparent thing about the lyrics, other than the irresistible title/chorus, is that they're inaudible, you *feel* their meaning from the (vaguely distorted) sound of the singer's voice and from their rhythmic expressiveness, and then slowly a few words here and there emerge from the sonic sludge, always perfectly appropriate to what you already know is being talked about, no surprises: "Why is the bedroom so cold/Turn away on your side?" "Resentment flies high/Where devotions won't grow." The power of love. The power it has to torture and destroy us by its seeming absence, by our inability to find and express the source of what we're feeling or not feeling. "There's a taste in my mouth." Yeah. The singer's flailing at something. And it's the very feebleness with which he flails that makes his performance so terrifyingly convincing.

Go figure. History records that Ian Curtis (Joy Division's vocalist) killed himself shortly before this single was released. The rest of the band survived and became New Order, rising from the ashes to dominate the incorporation of computer methodology into rhythm rock music in the U.K. 1980's. Myth. Gloom. Romance. Success. Influence. History loves this kind of stuff.

But records this perfect don't need history. You can discover them blindfolded and brainwashed, unaware of roots, context, personalities, categories, completely detached from time as we know it. Something reaches out of the music and grabs us. And pulls us down into it.

Into the darkness.

And it won't let go.

*First release:* Factory FAC 23 (U.K.), June 1980

# 84

## Yoko Ono

# *Walking on Thin Ice*

Listen without prejudice. Impossible, I know—every record comes to us complete with baggage, our preconceptions about the artist or the type of music, our expectations (positive and negative), even our unavoidable awareness of historical events, in this case the murder of the artist's husband the same day they finished making this single together. "The past weekend we had listened to the song all day and night. It was as if we were both haunted by the song. I remember I woke up in the morning and found John watching the sunrise and still listening to the song." John Lennon coproduced "Walking on Thin Ice" (with Yoko and Jack Douglas), and plays lead guitar and keyboards. This was his last record. It's a great one.

(If it didn't have Yoko's name on it, it would probably have been a top five record, U.S. and U.K. So it goes.)

It *is* Yoko's record, of course—she wrote it, she sings it, she conceived it and arranged it and inspired Lennon and Tony Levin (bass) and Andy Newmark (drums) and Hugh McCracken and Earl Slick (rhythm guitars) to reach extraordinary levels of intensity in their own performances. It's a record driven by spirit, by one woman's vision—in hindsight one can't help but believe that she felt the gathering force of the storm about to break, and (unconsciously, unerringly) seized the opportunity to capture it in music, one last burst of musical collaboration (hey, we got it right this time!) before the act broke up forever. Sometimes you can feel things and express them without yet knowing what they are. Music the rising breath of the creative. Precursor to a scream—

The sounds. Like the intentionally muddied vocals of "Love Will Tear Us Apart," the intricate patterns of (instrumental and vocal) screams in "Walking on Thin Ice," and the glorious bass/drum/rhythm figures that accompany and counterpoint them, represent a fresh statement, familiar yet revolutionary, a breakthrough. Great singles break through. This results partly from inventiveness, but more particularly from passion. In this medium (rock recording) artists are driven to create new sounds. They do this not primarily to be seen as innovators, but for a deeper reason: what they feel is not adequately expressed by the palette already available. Passion rages within. New colors, new sounds, allow the release of this passion into the open air.

Turn it up loud. You are in the studio. It's underground, of course, and no light gets in; but in the artists' imaginations this studio has two large picture windows, and they look out upon the whole world. Yoko is at her microphone, John perhaps in the control room fingering his unplugged guitar (overdubs later), and both of them and everyone else present are performing to an imagined audience of millions. No, more than millions, in a sense, because this imagined audience (felt, smelled, almost seen, just beyond that wall/window) is actually *everyone.* This is what I want to say to you, to each of you, all of you. "I may cry someday/But the tears will dry whichever way . . ." "Ai ai ai ai ai ai ai ai . . ."

There are many extraordinary transitions in this masterpiece of sonic textures, but two are critical: when the screams first come in, after "It'll be just a story" (the end of the regular verses), and then when the screams drop out again and the bass-and-percussion figure is heard front and center and alone, opening us out onto a new stage, which Yoko is about to enter singing/speaking only with voice (no words). She moans and then retches, and it works (it shouldn't but it does, listen without prejudice, an amazing performance), and leads (after another moan, and a little singing gargle) into the parable that frames the song (usually a bit has to recur to be considered a frame, but there's no other correct word for the role of this riveting recitation).

But back to the transitions. Each one brings us into another world. The song opens (as the rhythm figure comes in after the assault of the first notes), and opens, and opens again. Yoko's singing/screaming/speaking in the three parts of this tour de force is superb, but the song's true power arises from its willingness to let the rhythm section speak as fiercely and penetratingly as the vocalist. This is not about one person. It's a collective creation. A rock and roll record. Personification of a moment. A cry of pain and joy. From all of us in here to all of you out there. Thin ice. Watch out. Watch out.

*First release:* Geffen K 79202, February 1981

# 85 R.E.M.

## *Radio Free Europe*

Words that can almost (not quite) be heard have a funny way of stirring up feelings in us we can almost (not quite) identify.

This is not a song about Europe.

It is a song about music, the flow of music, the excitement in the fact that it just keeps coming, out of the air, the water, a song about nature overflowing with music like creeks in spring after a rainy winter. Enthusiasm & rapture. Along with an intriguing detachment: we're just here to bring you this news. Thanks for the opportunity to be of service. Hope you can understand our accents.

No. Yes. I mean, I can hardly understand a word, but your message comes through loud and clear. "Wake up, everybody." Yes. One of my favorite messages. So happy to hear it again.

Fecundity. Rock runs in cycles. As the cycles wear down, to the veterans the possibilities seem exhausted, running faster and wearier with less and less conviction in an ever-narrowing track. Meanwhile out in the boondocks somewhere, Athens Hawthorne Liverpool Tupelo, young turks are chomping at the bit, filled to bursting with innocent, revolutionary energy and ideas, pawing the ground, ready to bust out of the corral. Not even necessarily ambitious. Just full of love and creativity and hungry for life.

Jangling guitars. Roadrunner rhythm. Mumbled, mysterious vocals. Yeah, but what makes the difference, I think, what distinguishes this record as the beginning of yet another new age (long may they return), is a throwaway ten-second harmonic bridge about two-thirds of the way through, vocals even less identifiable than elsewhere, the R.E.M. change, floating, bizarre, an authentic break in the wall of reality, letting in a new kind of light. Perfect tangent to the melody, rhythm, and mood that charges consistent and breathless through every other instant of this debut indie single (hey we don't need no record company) (we're nobody we're inevitability we came to play and we're looking for gigs, got our name from rapid eye movement, sleep plus dreams, vocalist won't talk to anybody but hey the guitar player's a regular chatterbox). That bridge is the opening. Not any more wonderful than the rest of the record, but it gives it its connection to the eternal, the infinite, to Otherness in all its everchanging clothes of many colors. Welcome aboard.

"Calling out/in transit/calling out/in transit . . ."

R.E.M. arrives. Just as if they'd never left us. "The sound of mmmph mmmph radio's gonna stay . . ." (bomp bomp bomp)

Smiles on our faces. Here we go again.

*First release:* Hib-Tone 0001, July 1981

# 86

## Prince

# *When You Were Mine*

Not a hit. As we get toward the back end of this book, that is, closer to the present day, we find more and more great singles that didn't actually become hit records. This is unfortunate—why deprive the needy millions of the pleasures that could be available to them?—but not too surprising given the Big Money rules that govern the music biz in recent decades and the caution and conservatism (the important thing isn't having fun or even having a big hit; the most important thing is *staying in control*) that naturally result. These days a single (not just a promotional CD but something you actually think the public might buy copies of) is like a major investment, not to be entered into lightly. Go see the company banker and explain why this record will sell ("it's just like such-and-such that sold great last month" is almost the only acceptable answer) and maybe you'll get your loan.

"When You Were Mine," a natural easy water-off-a-duck's-back #1 hit single to my ears, was not even released as a 45 in the U.S. the year the album came out; a U.K. release is listed but it didn't make the top 75 and I've yet to find a copy. How come? Well most of the time we'll never know what bits of bad luck or what complexities of office politics got in the way of the manifest destiny of any given hot platter, but in this case it's an easy guess that the frank and outrageous sexuality of this young (not yet famous, not yet obviously bankable) artist's *Dirty Mind* album was the major stumbling block. "When You Were Mine" is a track from said album (along with, ahem, "Head," and "Sister"), and although in and of itself it's not really any more suggestive than plenty of tunes that were getting lotsa airplay, its association with *that* album tended to make lines like "you didn't have the decency to change the sheets" sound worse than they otherwise might have.

Whatever. Good reviews improved Prince's relationship with

his record company, and almost three years later a much more sexually graphic and almost equally wonderful single called "Little Red Corvette" hit the top 10 and broke Prince as a, like, artist with mass appeal. Some things are just meant to happen. Incredible perseverance combined with phenomenal talent and inventiveness does have a way of winning out in the end.

But anyway. A truly great record. The CD mix, at least on the early pressing I have, is all wrong—too slow, not punchy enough, the penetrating (mind-breaking) power of the keyboard scream in the middle of the song is almost completely lost, all sorts of sound magic audible on cassette and lp are missing, digitaled out, not home today—buy yourself a cassette, since lp's are now collector's items, and turn up the volume and just enjoy enjoy enjoy. How could he possibly get such a groove going while playing all the instruments himself? I don't understand it but the evidence is incontrovertible. And what gives the record its special edge (why it appears on the list over such deserving contenders as "Kiss" and "Corvette" and "Erotic City") is its conviction, the authenticity and depth and subtlety of the feelings expressed by the singer through the persona of this fictional character. (Prince a great story-weaver, with emphasis on the sexual vignette.)

Obsession. Here it is again. You really got me. I don't got you.

And I like it. That's what he's saying, clear as day. As much as I accepted and even ignored your tartiness while we were together, now that you've moved out it just really turns me on. Love you more than I did. And we the listeners can feel it. This guy's crazy. Recognizable, familiar crazy. Gooseflesh.

Structural note: I never noticed this till I wrote out the lyrics, but there are twelve lines in the first verse (prior to first chorus), eight lines in the second verse (great climactic squeal after second chorus), and four lines in the third verse. Things speed up. The hook keeps coming sooner.

Play it again. Groove won't quit. Madness won't quit. Great melodic/rhythmic magic won't quit. Singer's magnificent sense of humor won't quit (those who call him humorless reveal themselves as earless and funnyboneless, methinks). Pleasure won't quit. Song and performance endure, penetrate, entertain, nourish, give pleasure. Over and over. Play it again. Some records just have their sights set on a more far-reaching picture of what a hit is. Endurance. Penetration. Fuck the charts. Let's go the distance.

*First release:* Warner 49808, September 1981

# 87

## Grandmaster Flash and the Furious Five

# *The Message*

Perfect title. When someone said, "the truth shall set you free," he wasn't just talking about good news. This record leapt out of the airwaves in 1982 with a message of anger, frustration, and despair. It describes the dark side of ghetto life without sentimentality or compromise. The sound of the record is as stark and compelling as the story the speaker tells. A new sound: lyrics spoken rather than sung, dominant rhythm located in the vocals not the backup, primary musical accompaniment not by a band but by a "dj" creating eerie, distinctive, repetitive sounds by manipulating phonograph needles and turntables, snatching bits from other records and making music from the sounds thus obtained. Rap. "The Message" was hardly the first rap record, but its sonic power, its universal accessibility (after the first shock, you find yourself pulled in forcefully), and the astonishing immediacy of its lyrics combined to make it the official announcement of the start of something truly new. A fresh musical form, the first in many decades that would succeed in asserting an existence entirely independent from rock and roll and the pop/soul mainstream. And a new communications medium: rap U.S.A., the voice of the black underclass, getting out the news that isn't carried by the other wire services. "Don't/push/me/'cause I'm/close to the edge/I'm/trying/not to/lose/my head." Dangerous honesty, claustrophobic and depressing and yet full of the exultation that comes when forbidden repressed information is expressed out loud. Terrifying and liberating. A big stink. And a breath of fresh air.

Strange that the record is not the work, as it seems when it comes sizzling out of the radio, of one angry articulate young man. If there's an individual who bears primary responsibility for this example of collective creation, this explosion of new language from deep in the collective unconscious, it has to be

Sylvia Robinson, co-owner of a tiny New Jersey record label called Sugarhill. In 1956 she collaborated on a classic sing-talk record that could easily have been in this book, Mickey and Sylvia's "Love Is Strange." She had another hit, "Pillow Talk," in 1973, and in 1979 it was her inspiration to put together the Sugar Hill Gang (out on the cutting edge because she paid attention when her son told her what the other kids were into) and produce the first successful rap single, "Rapper's Delight." Then in 1982 she got excited about a song written by rapper Duke Bootee and insisted, over Flash's objections, that Grandmaster Flash and the Furious Five record it. She and Bootee and vocalist/rapper Melle Mel (Flash was not the singer but the dj, one of the most brilliant creators of sound collages on the hip-hop scene; he admits the song scared him, and that they only agreed to record it because Robinson promised it wouldn't be a single) fine-tuned the lyrics, and the group cut the record; Robinson changed her mind and put it out as a twelve-inch single (a new format created during the disco seventies for dance-oriented records) and it sold half a million copies in the first month.

"It's like a jungle sometimes, it makes me wonder, how I keep from going under." Random violence, fearing for your life as you walk down the street, children and adults equally trapped in an environment of relentless physical and emotional oppression ("I can't take the smell, can't take the noise/Got no money to move out, I guess I got no choice") ("Rats in the front room, roaches in the back") ("Crazy lady, living in a bag, eating out of garbage pails"), young people with absolutely no attractive role models except pimps and pushers ("Driving big cars, spending 20s and 10s/And you want to grow up to be just like them"), the hopelessness of school, no future, prospects of jail, slavery to drugs, slavery to prostitution, early death, death and mayhem to friends and loved ones . . . This is not good news. This is not a feel-good record, except insofar as you're already living with the knowledge that this is reality and you're eager for the truth to get out. If there's any hope it begins with honesty. This record shames rock and roll, confronts it with its limitations. "That's not music, it's noise!" say the Beatles fans, Elvis fans, Led Zeppelin fans, like their parents and their parents' parents before them. Uh huh. Kill that messenger. Nail him up. Shut out his awful bleating.

Not rock and roll, but a great rock record anyway because it rips away the mask, both lyrically and musically. We are not the crown of creation. There are other ways to tell the truth. And a whole lot of truth still left to be told.

*First release:* Sugarhill SHL 117, July 1982

# 88 Modern English

## *I Melt with You*

Can't trust the charts anymore. I don't mean you ever could, in terms of accuracy or anything, but as we move into the '80's and '90's the dislocations get more bizarre. One primary characteristic of a major hit, especially in the '50's and '60's, was that it was all over the airwaves and so, like it or not, if you listened to the radio you heard it constantly—and years later, you and lots of other people would associate that moment in time with that song.

But then radio fragmented. Talk took over, for one thing—a very unhealthy sign—while music radio itself split into a score of different marketing segments, all overlapping in weird ways but stretched out so much that traditional "top 40" radio (the hits) became actually just another small subgroup, and if you didn't happen to be a fourteen-year-old white girl, the #1 song in the land for five weeks in a row would probably come and go without you ever knowing it existed.

Just as well (and if you'd rather watch music than listen to it, you could remedy the "problem" somewhat by zoning out for hours in front of MTV). But it has become harder and harder for the sort of record that cuts across fixed audience lines (most of the stuff in this book) and just makes direct contact with its delighted listeners, to find a home. And most surprising, those records that we do some of us remember as having been omnipresent at a particular moment, may not actually have been "hits" in the narrow definition offered by the modern charts. "The Message" was heard by most of us and sold its several million, but it's not in *The Billboard Book of Top 40 Hits.* Neither is "Blue Monday" by New Order—didn't make the U.S. Top 40, and only got to #9 in the U.K., although it was one of the largest-selling and most-heard singles of the '80's. The chart-makers can explain, of course: black sales don't count on the top 40 list (don't like the color of their money?), dance records get put on different lists, twelve-inch singles get put on different lists, stations that play album tracks don't count when figuring out what's a radio hit, even if they also play singles, etc ad nauseam.

Case in point: "I Melt with You" by Modern English, voted one of the five greatest songs of all time this year ('92) by the listeners of the radio station my son tunes in, the sort of hit single that keeps the whole catalog of an otherwise forgettable band alive a decade past their high point. The CD sleeve says the single "reached the top of the alternative charts in both the U.S. and the U.K." In the U.S. I guess that means "college radio"; in the U.K. I don't know what it means, but *British Hit Singles* says the record never made the top 75 in a country where from a U.S. perspective the charts seem packed with records that are strictly consigned to the "alternative" heap over here.

Well. Sorry to take up all the space with such blathering, but the point is a simple one: "I Melt with You" is classic pop, instantly likable and long endurable, the sort of record rock and roll's empire has been built upon. But to the historian browsing the published lists of "all" hit songs of the era, it never existed. This is not necessarily a bad thing. Invisibility (especially omnipresent invisibility) has definite advantages.

The words are mostly silly. That doesn't matter. So are most of the words to "Satisfaction." What matters, just as with that ancient venerable "hit," is the tension/release (the hook) as we move from verse to chorus, one silly but inspired phrase in the bridge ("the future's open wide") and the cute bit of musical world-stopping that follows it the second time, the way the instruments sound together (tone/rhythm) as the song starts, and most of all the key phrase, neatly anchored by a reference in the verse that confirms that it is fucking we're talking about, as well as all the moments in our lives that have a, ah, somewhat similar feeling: "I'll stop the world and melt with you." Not the words. The *phrase,* meaning lyrical phrase, melodic phrase (including chord change), rhythmic phrase, phrase as release from lyrical/melodic/rhythmic tension built up earlier and phrase as tension (will I get to hear this and feel this good feeling again?) promising to be released in some future instant.

Timeless. Like fucking. But so clean and pure. Sheer fantasy. Stop the world. Thank you. Don't mind if I do. Play it again please.

*First release:* 4ad (U.K.), November 1982

# 89

U2

## *New Year's Day*

Romance is where you find it. No, not only. It's also where you create it. That's the secret of U2: they are dramatists with a nose for that which gives life color, texture, depth. And one more thing: the great hopeless romantic in the group is not Bono (though he plays the part well). It's Dave Evans. The lead guitar. The Keith. The difference. The Edge.

Colors. This amazing single is not on the *War* album, so if you're a Yank you've probably never heard it. It's a clever edited variant of the album track, seven seconds taken out of the intro, a minute forty excised from the ending, and then a few vocal lines added by electronic cut-and-paste so that the record fades with Bono singing, five times instead of twice, "I . . . will be with you again." Quite different from fading, as the longer track does, with "Nothing changes on New Year's Day."

A single can have an impact an album track can never have, simply because it stands alone. (Too bad this unity of purpose and focus has been at least temporarily spoiled by CD/cassette singles with more than one song on a side. Pray for a return to form.) This record communicates *feeling.* It does this through tone of voice, through pulling the bass line forward until it dominates the melody, through symphonic noises that sound like street traffic from a city window, through guitar lines played on keyboards and bursts of percussion on the guitar that echo and magically frame the haunting bass riff and the ecstatic regularity of the drumming. There is a sense of motion here that is a brush moving confidently on a large canvas, filling in surprising details and achieving remarkable textures as it sweeps by. The Edge is the brush man. He throws up his mural, and turns to his front man & poet to provide the caption and make the meanings more and less evident. Front man responds with inspired, sympathetic genius this time out. Images and feelings. He tosses them out at us, spins them around us, reels us in. We project ourselves into the mural.

Turn the volume down and listen again. Okay, now turn it way up. What is the song about? It's about the romance of feeling connected (painfully, vulnerably, gloriously) to the world and to these times. I read in *Rolling Stone* (March 14, 1985) that "New Year's Day" is "a song about the Soviet domination of Poland." How does the journalist know? No doubt read it in an interview. And because on New Year's Day 1982, the year the song was written and recorded, unionism and the vision of an independent future were being crushed in Poland by the movement of Soviet troops over the border. But the song defies literal interpretation. "A crowd has gathered, black and white"—the image evoked is not Poland at all but something occurring in racially-mixed London or in the United States. "Torn in two" evokes Ireland. "I want to be with you/Be with you night and day" personalizes it fiercely, inner world merged with outer world; the best songs come from this sort of impulse.

Romance. This performance echoes in the brain, the heart. It is just the right length, just the right combination of beauty and abrasiveness, just the right mixture of silence and articulation and noise. It was U2's first hit in England. Easy to forget that they were (and are) one of the last great singles bands. Put out five singles prior to release of their first lp. Still offer their fans previously unreleased B-sides. Still capable of making a song like "One" or "Who's Gonna Ride Your Wild Horses?" that, heard alone, soars far beyond the limits of the album that tries to contain and enclose it.

Romance found in the newspaper, in the momentary sense of identification, in the very lack of hope that grays the heart and then provokes some sort of chemical or spiritual response. A response in sound. Colors of sound. Colors of conviction. When U2 do the song live it's the single version. Because this is where it all comes together. Three minutes and fifty-three seconds. Theme song for an era. "Nothing changes . . ." True and not true. Find a spark of romance and make something out of it. A bonfire. A rallying point. New sounds, new textures, new colors. A sense of purpose. A sense of loss. "I . . . will be with you again." Hey, we're just a rock band. But nevertheless. A sense of belonging.

*First release:* Island UWIP 6846 (U.K.), January 1983

# 90 George Clinton

## *Atomic Dog*

Okay. One of the things rock and roll in general, and my experience of writing this book in particular, is about, is EDUCATION. I mean, as I said somewhere else, I'm an idiot—there are so many worthwhile things I know next to nothing about that it's a wonder I can even show my face in public. Funk, for example, is not one of my strong suits. But I'd like to imagine I'm not too stubborn to learn. "Atomic Dog" got nominated for the list when I read a comment by Chuck D. (of Public Enemy) in a 1990 *Rolling Stone:* "This is every rapper's favorite record East, West, North or South. When you heard it you just had to move." Okay. Better check it out. I did, and loved it. Or did I? Came time to write about it and I wasn't sure anymore. Uh oh. Problem. The rules of this game require unshakable conviction, unending undying passion enthusiasm and allegiance. Gotta *love* it, can't just be terrifically impressed. When subjectivity's the only standard, honesty about one's subjectivity is absolutely paramount. So if I have doubts about a record, I listen over and over and either rediscover my passion unequivocably or else drop it from the book.

But every now and then there's a record that won't drop. It insists that I learn something. It teaches me (and hey I can be a very resistant student) how to listen. Education. At the end of this process I may or may not love the record, and so it may or may not stay on the list. But at least I've started learning a new musical language.

Same thing happens when you listen to the radio, if you're lucky enough to actually find a station that's programmed by human beings who love the music they're playing, or when you give your heart to artists like Talking Heads or U2 or Prince or Los Lobos who don't just make the same album over and over, who keep opening their hearts to new musical territory and do their best to drag their listeners along with them. Rock and roll, if we use that phrase to connote the root identity of the multiracial U.S/U.K. popular music that has somehow retained some sense of itself for almost forty years now, is inclusive and expansive. At its worst it turns other musical forms into marketable mush. At its best it provokes ambitious artists to create universal language, via songs and records and performances that surprise and delight and leave old prejudices in the dust.

Challenging (actually, obliterating) musical prejudices is George Clinton's stock in trade. He goes after the basic ground rules of song structure and turns them inside out—no verse/chorus, lots of repetition but no recognizable repeating pattern, either lyrical or melodic—"Atomic Dog" doesn't even have what I'd call a rhythmic pattern that repeats, just one pulsing rhythm that beats steady and strange throughout, collecting fragments of melody and lyric around it, unity not of narrative but of theme. A song about dogs, or maybe about being a dog, or— Whoops, almost had it there, now it got away again.

"Why must I feel like that?/Why must I chase the cat?" Good question. "Bow wow wow yippie yo yippie yay." Good answer, though the real answer is also "Nothing but the dog in me." A song about the dog in me. Definition of funk. It's not even precisely obvious which voice is George Clinton, that is, the primary narrator. Everything's turned sideways in terms of song as we know it. And yet it all sticks together brilliantly.

Some kind of dividing line. A #1 record on the black charts, famous among musicians and music-lovers everywhere, but even with a great video it couldn't break the (white) Top 40. "The Message" and "Atomic Dog" and all their progeny could easily have been rock and roll if rock and roll were still as ready to grow and learn as it used to was. Instead—and maybe this is for the best—there's a new music out there, funk, rap, hip-hop, too big and too different to ever be assimilated now, no matter how popular it gets.

Do I love this record? Yeah. It's a great one. But it makes me sad. Never thought I'd see the day when I'd have trouble picking up some new tricks—

*First release:* Capitol 5201, January 1983

# 91 The Pretenders

## *Middle of the Road*

Noise. A good song has a tightly wound spring at the center of it, and when you touch it, it comes apart, flinging itself at you at high velocity. In all directions. Or it touches your spring, and you fly apart. Noise. Excitement. Release of tension. Joyous disorder. Out of control. Wow, I *like* that. Give me a moment to rewind my soul and let's go on this adventure again.

Chrissie's voice is the vehicle. And her mind's the engine. That's why the words are important, you know—they drive the voice, empower it, give it hooks with which to grab on tight to singer and listener both, grab 'em by their thoughts and you unleash their feelings, chords melody beat and rhythmic structure all aid in this seduction, this immersion, but you know the mind's the great resister and when the right words capture mind and bind it to voice, then music and rhythm if they're great, if they're right, can move in on every sensory level and whoosh! we've got lift-off, tweeeee! that tightly wound spring is unwinding, bam crash! we're falling down stairs.

Signal to noise. It's a ratio. A relationship. Too much signal and we're trapped in thought, lose the beat, too rational, no feelings. Too much noise and we lose the beat another way, no pattern, no hook, no way to hang on and ride the noise, no connection. We want to ride, and what we ride in rock and roll is the ratio, the sine wave, the constantly moving point where meaning and chaos meet, touch, kiss, interact, and fight, spitting joyously at each other, hooks deep in contradictions, trying to come apart, disengage, let go, but bound together for these wild memorable seconds by the mathematics of momentum, like a rock in a whirling sling, because it is held it builds up a frightening power.

Signal to noise. This is a song about the primal fear of every rock and roller: being swallowed by pop. Loss of noise. Easy listening. "The middle of the road/Is trying to find me/I'm standing in the middle of life with my plans behind me." This woman is wise. And honest. With poet quickness and economy she turns the meaning of the title phrase, again and yet again, allowing a few words to tell a flurry of different stories. The chorus is purely sexual, lending dignity and authentic lustfulness to the Beatles' schoolboyish refrain "Why Don't We Do It in the Road?" Second verse is political, global, delightfully fierce and right on target: "When you own a big chunk of the bloody Third World, the babies just come with the scenery." Ohio girl observes London's immigrant slums, and sees and summarizes the economic manipulation for personal profit that brings about these conditions. "In the middle of the road, you see the darndest things . . ."

There's a wonderful count-off bridge that swallows itself (the song is patterned after a Rolling Stones B-side, I mean that's the aesthetic that's reached for here, and achieved brilliantly), and then the third verse paints a vivid scene of rock star autobiography (excellent follow-up to two previous fabulous Pretenders' singles in this vein, "Brass in Pocket" and "Back on the Chain Gang"): "I can't get from the cab to the curb without some little jerk on my back." The middle of the road's a public place. Her words and her delivery are deadly: "Don't harass me can't you tell/I'm going home I'm sick of sell/I'm not the cat I used to be/I've got a kid I'm 33" and then as if to gloriously and teasingly contradict it all, a display of the sassy intelligent sexiness that made her a star in the first place . . . "C'mon baby, get in the road!", followed by an irresistible low spitting purr to make sure we know she's as much cat as ever. She is.

And the relentless rock-and-roll-ness of it. Makes you want to dance. Scream. Burst open. Play guitar. Play drums. Be in a band. Be the singer. Be in the crowd that watches her get out of the taxi. Beat your fists against the air. This is intellectual headbanging music, classic Stones grunge, wonderful rhythmic slugfest, noisy, exciting, not middle of the road at all. But that sweet abyss of mediocrity is always beckoning . . .

*First release:* Sire 29444, December 1983

# 92 Prince

## *When Doves Cry*

"What if every radio and TV and everybody in their house were playing this song at the same time, all over the world?" This question, asked by my four-year-old stepson as he listened to "When Doves Cry" on the car radio, sums up the importance of the single for me: it is one of the great unifying objects of our era. A hit record cuts across all cultural and social barriers to bring us together (listening to the same recording, touching the same talisman at the same moment and thus touching each other)—to make us vitally aware of our connectedness in space and time. "This is what it sounds like . . ." Yes. For a moment, we agree. It is a good place to begin.

What's astonishing about Prince is that it's not hard to believe that he could come up with another five-weeks-at-number-one huge universal hit single whenever he wanted to. (If ever.) No one since the Beatles has given this impression. Prince is very able (as he demonstrates in the film this song was written for) to play the role of the mythic artist, plugged into some immense creative force. "When Doves Cry" sparkles with freshness and power. It seems to come out of nowhere with an insistent, irresistible familiarity. "You've never heard anything like me before," it says to each of us, "but you've *almost* heard me a thousand times." Shock of recognition. Music as personal news, as truth, as a vehicle of awakening. This song is about, and simultaneously it offers an experience of, ecstatic union.

"Why do we scream at each other?" This question is not often asked, and it takes us into mature realms of relationship—conflict, tenderness, pain, vulnerability, reconciliation—not often touched on in rock and roll, where pain is virtually always about separation from the loved one, rather than about the challenge of being present (with each other, with our pasts and our parents who live inside us, with our imperfections and immaturity, our neediness, our angers). Song structure is (as so often with great singles) simple and natural and utterly (invisibly) unorthodox: eight-line verse followed by eight-line chorus, second verse cuts off after four lines and goes back to chorus, which repeats after a very brief instrumental break. Resolution/ fade. Partly because of this structure, but probably more for reasons that can never be explained, Inspiration, Mystery, the song has the impact of a fragment of a much larger work, a work never to be heard directly but only felt through the presence of this fragment, an interrupted or half-remembered dream, like Coleridge's "Kubla Khan." And of course the obvious heart of the record's power, its genius, its evidence of having come from some higher deeper unknown-yet-profoundly-familiar place, is the beat. The sound. The beat. The beat is the sound, or vice versa, enters directly through our pores, nerve endings moving muscles even before the ecstatic message reaches and floods our brain. Innovation. The word seems lame for what's accomplished here. No one could simply invent this. Rather, the artist has opened a door in reality, found a hidden passageway, torn open the entrance to another world. Four-year-olds, twelve-year-olds, fifteen-year-olds, forty-four-year-olds respond instantly, intuitively, bodies moving, hearts lifting, voices singing along, no need to understand, pied piper music, speaking to the child in us, nursery rhymes, how can a song about the problem of violence in sexual relationships speak to the child in us? Very very directly. The violence that lives in, comes out of, ourselves. Revelation. Acknowledgment. Tenderness. Liberation. What if a beat, a rhythm, were so appealing, so universal, that it spoke immediately and unerringly to each of us, cutting through all resistance and calling us to dance together? Would the world be healed? Perhaps not. But how extraordinary that a song could even bring us to contemplate the possibility.

This is not contrivance. This is, um, art. A moment of contact, through the artist, with some primal creative force. Shock of recognition. This is what it sounds like. "Animals strike curious poses." We are looking into our own private known but seldom spoken of intimate reality, and as we look we see through to something larger. Ecstatic union. Universal awakening. Questions without answers. A feeling of awe.

*First release:* Warner 29286, June 1984

# 93

U2

# *Pride (In the Name of Love)*

Not subtle. Why should it be? The whole purpose of this record is to make a big noise. Martin Luther King is a kind of prop, an appropriate one. He is made to stand for something. The apotheosis of the common man. An excuse to shout really loud and beat the drum as hard and straight ahead as possible, guitars ringing gloriously all around, filling the sky with fireflowers. "One man! One man! One man!" they shout over and over, alternating with the slurred homonym "Once more! Once more!" If this song were about anyone *but* MLK it would probably be terrifying.

Never mind. It works.

Big noise. If you've ever been a parent, you've seen a toddler pull all the pots and pans out of the kitchen cupboard and bang on them joyously and wildly. Instinctive impulse. Blissful fulfillment. What is it that's so satisfying about our own cacophonies? Never mind. U2 has decided to make the loudest single they're capable of, and the most passionately political-romantic, kind of like the entire *War* album in one song, just to get it out of their system. And they've invited you to scream along.

What does it take to wake us up, to cut through our considerations, to make us eager and hungry to be alive? The *I Ching* says, "Religious forces are needed to overcome the egotism that divides men. They must be shaken by a religious awe in the face of eternity—stirred with an intuition of the one creator of all living beings, and united through the strong feeling of fellowship experienced in the ritual of divine worship." This is the third in a trio of great U2 singles that address this issue head on, in a nonsectarian fashion, intuitively and exuberantly and unabashedly pursuing those feelings in themselves, in us, strong enough to make possible and make sense of the extraordinary emotion of fellowship felt during a live rock and roll show. The other two are "I Will Follow" (1980) and "Gloria" (1981), and all three in their distinctive ways are sonic assaults, an attempt to break down the barriers that divide us by use of direct musical force. Storm the battlements. Go for the jugular.

There is an obvious lyrical/thematic/spiritual thread linking these songs together, but, in the best rock and roll tradition, the lyrics function not as essays or thoughts but as images, touchstones, rallying points. "If you walk away walk away walk away walk away, I will follow." "If I have anything, I give it to you." Images of feelings. The first two are love songs, I/Thou. "Pride" takes these feelings of love and collectivizes them, third person singular impersonal ("one man come in the name of love") present tense relentlessly throughout the song until the last two lines of the third verse, which suddenly (through the impact of the rifle shot, the martyrdom) awakens into second person, implicit I/Thou, awareness of self, of history (specific past tense), and also introduces the existence of the Other, "they": "Free at last, they took your life/They could not take your pride." Very clever, that one climactic word as the title of the song, the hook, focusing point, followed by the now supercharged screaming along of the chorus: "In the *name* of *love . . .*" If this song were about Jesus or Bobby Sands no one would touch it with a ten-foot pole, but the choice of King is perfect (and sincere, I hasten to add; U2 couldn't begin to pull this stuff off if they weren't utterly and unmistakably and almost pathetically sincere about it), the point being it almost allows us to forget that it's all our Jesus buttons (mythology of our civilization, regardless of our personal "beliefs") that are being pushed.

Anyway, the main thing is, the words don't get in the way. The power is in the noise. And it is original, unique, inventive, at times (paradoxically) extremely subtle noise, new sounds, new methods, incredible creativity. Attack! Drive! The real triumph of the performance is the formless instrumental stretch in the middle, pure essence of U2, pounding, hammering, ringing, echoing, humming, safe heart space at the center of the relentless assault, not less intense but simply open to whatever the listener needs to project onto it (like the "make a circle" section in "I Will Follow").

Pride can be a bad thing, but here it is exalted as the most noble of human conditions. Not inappropriately. A great song is the reflection not of its creators but of its listeners. Notice how this record makes you feel. Be wary. Be worried even—these passions within us are not altogether good news. But notice also how great it feels to be this fucking awake.

*First release:* Island IS 202 (U.K.), September 1984

# 94

## Tears for Fears

### *Shout*

I want to tell you everything. This is a feeling. It is perhaps, in a certain way, the most exciting feeling I have ever felt; and this record evokes it, bathes me in it, and expresses it for me. "Shout. Shout. Let it all out." I feel this surge of desire and wholeness rising in me and I am thrilled. "Come on! I'm talking to you. Come on . . ." I love this feeling. I probably can't ever tell you everything, but the desire to do so is my fondest possession. Raise the stakes. Up the ante. Let it all out. I imagine I'm on the trembling edge of doing so. I can hear the sound of it, all the complex glorious rhythmic and melodic rising intensity of it. It's talking to me, with me, for me—

I love this record.

I want to let it out. I know I'm not alone. The words, "These are the things I can do without," affirm that an important part of what needs to be let out is anger, but the song's triumph is its union of anger with all passion, with love, with the fiery need to communicate that is somehow essential to our survival. Roland Orzabal has acknowledged that one of the things he was thinking about as he wrote these words and tried to give birth to the music he heard in them, was the outrage he felt (along with so many other people circa 1983) about the installment of American nuclear missiles in the U.K. Specific issue. But not intellectual. Visceral. Feeling comes first. And in that feeling (and the awareness that it is shared) comes self-awareness. It comes in a wave, surge, rising tide, breaks on the shore and rises again and again, crescendo, forceful and beautiful, the feeling of knowing oneself to have feelings, and knowing even for a moment that these feelings have value, are worthy of existence. They belong here. I belong here. Hello. I assert myself. I celebrate myself. This is not egotism. This is rhapsody a la Walt Whitman or John Donne, awakening, self-awareness, the awakening of Godhood from within the individual, breaking the chains that the ego has placed around it. Shout! I am. It is the collective reality that this assertion expresses that gives it its power, but this collective consciousness is expressed through individual voices. "We are" is a powerful statement. But real awakening, in our time, our culture, is found in the paintings of Van Gogh or the hypotheses of Albert Einstein or the vocalizations of Billie Holiday, and the text of this awakening is always the same: "I am."

Mystery. The specific purpose of music is to serve as a collective repository of mystery, a public well, available to everyone, privately or publicly, at any hour of the day. And what is mysterious is not the words, or the musical parts those various instruments are playing, but the spaces between words and music, between sounds and the "I" hearing those sounds, between verbal image and sonic image, between "I" here and "I" in you over there. What is mysterious is the feelings these sounds can arouse in me, this evidence that I'm alive.

I don't mean to trivialize it by talking about it. Tears for Fears are at their most articulate in the cataclysmic instrumental passage at the center of this song (returning with even greater ferocity just prior to the seven-inch fade). Mystery shouts alongside the urban jackhammers here, screams to be heard above the traffic, to obliterate the traffic and create a clear channel between I and thou. Rock and roll at its most essential. Turn up the volume. Open the floodgates. Listen. Here it comes. I'm talking to you. I don't care who Tears for Fears are. The point is, for a moment they grabbed the eternal fire and lit up the sky with it, and that moment was immortalized in vinyl. Find a phonograph. Listen to this record. It captures something. It makes a difference. It burns with a mysterious brightness.

*First release:* Mercury IDEA 8 (U.K.), November 1984

# 95 Tramaine

## *Fall Down*

Here's one that should—like "When Doves Cry" or "Peggy Sue"—belong to everyone, but it doesn't. Yet. It certainly could. To hear it is to be transported, immediately, just about inevitably, taken out of your enmeshments and complications and back to the core of your being. Universal. Irresistible. A #1 dance record, top 10 on the urban (black music) charts, but that means that even folks who were listening to what passed for top 40 radio in 1985 may never have heard it. Too bad. This record is essence. "Fall down/On me/Let your spirit fall down on me/In my heart in my soul in my mind all over me . . ." Tramaine is Tramaine Hawkins, gospel singer from a famous Oakland, California, gospel family, who let herself be talked into recording a gospel dance record, written and produced by Robert Wright and Vassal Benford, with a rhythm track that won't quit and a lyrical image that succeeds in uniting apocalyptic Christianity and the ecstasy of the dance floor, "fall down" (magic words when dancing) "spirit of love fall down on me." With a vocal bold enough to shatter the defenses of the most recalcitrant sinner, and a rhythmic underpinning (special extended mix, hey this is the *ne plus ultra* of twelve-inch singles) that demands that you keep moving till you lose everything, all that stuff you brought in with you, those ideas, gone, that resistance, gone, that resignation, all gone, just dancing your heart out like you really are the person who lives in this body and nothing else matters. Spirit. Fall. Down. On me! This is the record every modern singer and rock band has always wanted to make. They edited it for the album and turned it to porridge. Oh well. Find that twelve-inch. Thirty years from now it will be as famous (or as forgotten; who knows the future?) as "Whole Lot of Shakin' Going On." A black disc, an object, object of wonder, bit of encoded information, capable of invoking miracles. Dance to it (eight minutes and seventeen seconds, plus the sixty-seven second a cappella coda that follows on the same side of the record). See what happens.

"I *need* you I *need* you I *need* you . . ." Insistence and passion. The black Baptist church is a kind of dance floor itself, but sanctified, and when we speak in tongues and writhe with passion, there's no music to hide the nakedness of our movements and our vocalizations. Just you and me, spirit, and somewhere out there those who witness and make the space for our fellowship. But something similar is going on as we silence our tongues and dance beside strangers to that throbbing bass-line till almost dawn. Convergence. Awakening. Release. And is there in a way something sacrilegious about being able to take this record out of the club, play it at home, divorce it from its context, from the unspoken ecstatic fellowship that gives it purpose? I don't know. I don't think so. I don't go to the clubs or the churches, mostly, though I deeply respect what goes on for the truly devoted in either sanctum. I'm a child of the phonograph, for better or worse, take the object home and create my own ceremony. With a partner sometimes, but sometimes I just have to let this scream be from and for me alone.

The rhythm. The voice. The background voices. This is a long, rich, complex record, I get lost every time, and yet it is so rooted in basics. Simple elements. Built up on themselves till thought breaks down and something larger emerges. Comes out to play. To dance. To scream. To beg for apocalypse. What a strange idea. As if I want this entire city, this world of complications, to fall down on me and set me free of it. Jesus as Siva. I don't know. I just feel it. Tramaine's voice. That guitar riff, that amazing rhythm track. Something is trembling on the edge here. This is what we listen to music for, isn't it? The hope (prayer, entreaty) that spirit will descend and take me out of this place. We want to be transported. We want deliverance. We want truth. We want someone somewhere to keep all those promises. We want to feel like dancing.

*First release:* A&M SP-12146, September 1985

# 96 Peter Gabriel

## *Sledgehammer*

Sounds dumb but grows on you. What would we do without songs like this? (I guess the question has already been answered by the proliferation of "oldies" stations on the radio—without a steady infusion of new hits sufficiently universal in their appeal to cut across racial, cultural, and generational divisions, we'll just play the old ones absolutely to death . . . some more. This is not a healthy trend.) "Sledgehammer" walks the razor's edge of being absolutely generic—thud-thud big band rhythms and boastful sexual metaphors recycled from a hundred forgotten blues songs—and comes away with its inventiveness and charm intact. Getting better all the time, in fact. How does he do that?

With genuine affection. Here's an odd theory: in order for a song to be truly likable, it has to like itself. I've probably said this before (hope so), but one of the main things rock and roll is about is having fun. Get too far from this simple truth (oh it's easy to stray) and we break the law of attraction. Break that law (freedom to join the party or not, depending solely on the looks on the faces of the partygoers and whether you're feeling sociable this afternoon) and next thing you know there's a cop on every corner, telling us which parties we belong at and what records we really like. Such things, they explain solemnly, must not be left to chance. Yeah. The capsule history of all addictions is: freedom equals fun equals popularity equals profit equals slavery. Buy this record, kid, if you know what's good for you.

(This book, like any sincere statement of personal affection, could be dangerous if it falls into the wrong hands. If you find a copy in the possession of the cultural police, you have my permission to burn it.)

Good drum sound. The title, "Sledgehammer," tells us in a sense that what the song is about is the thrill of this drum sound, the satisfaction of really coming down hard on the beat.

I mean, it's a joke. A friendly joke, a sexual joke, a wry expression of self-mockery and joy. "Going to build that power/Build, build up that power, hey/I've been feeding the rhythm . . ." The next logical step, a great video with the singer as a cartoon of himself, is not just effective promotion but the appropriate or inevitable extension of the basic inspiration (variation on "find a riff and ride it"), more fun, hard work but hard work *is* fun when the momentum's right and that also is suggested in the title—"All you do is call me/I'll be anything you need." I'm not saying it'll be effortless. I'm saying the way you inspire me to make this effort is what turns me on about you. And vice versa. Play it again.

Grows on me why? Some kind of brainwashing, I mean it's like I get calibrated to its rhythm, various subtle adjustments so that by the third time in a row (or close proximity) I hear it I'm attuned, very gently addicted maybe, my pulse influenced by and responding to the rhythm, even my mind subtly tuned in to this particular wavelength of charm and wordplay, this angle of incidence, a particular (likable, adoptable) attitude. Got me. And I like being gotten. Phooey on a world where experiences are had only once. I like repetition. I like, um, courtship. Give and take. Accumulation of kinetic energy. Getting to know each other. Growing together.

Good tone of voice. Great arrangement. Is there such a thing as subtle obviousness? This performance is full of the stuff. God, I'm really starting to like it. A hit. Infectious, that's what it is. Silly song. Five or six like this in the course of a year, and everybody'd start listening to top 40 radio again. "This amusement never ends." I wish.

Where'd it come from? Where'd it go? No one knows. But hey, it was fun while it lasted.

*First release:* Virgin PGS 1 (U.K.), April 1986

# 97

## R.E.M.

# *The One I Love*

Things are seldom what they seem. This song for a loved one is actually about the absence of love (I think). The sound of the song, which is most of what makes it so appealing, is not an "R.E.M. sound" at all but rather a tribute to (or rip-off of) Neil Young. After twenty-odd years he *owns* these chords, these changes, this guitar sound, and this-guitar-sound-combined-with-this-drum-sound. I love the very identifiable special sound that R.E.M. owns (traces of which can be heard on the last entry in this book, Nirvana's "Smells Like Teen Spirit"), so it seems strange that this quite atypical R.E.M. single ends up on my list, until I remind myself that the single isn't here to represent the group or my enthusiasm for their oeuvre; it's here for itself alone, because it is one of those rare great recordings that has the power to pull me in, and hold me, and bring me back again and again, wanting more. I'm gonna call the request hotline. I'm gonna go down and buy myself a copy.

"This one goes out to the one I love . . ." This hypnotic line starts and ends every verse; it's also the second line, except that "I love" becomes "I've left behind." The third line is the twist: "A simple prop to occupy my time." Oh thanks a lot. The chorus is one word, "Fire," stretched out and imploded (with some other word-sound interpolated in the middle) so its impact is sonic rather than verbal—for the first weeks of my love affair with the record I thought he was saying "I am!" There are three verses, each exactly the same, except that third time around the third line is modified thus: "Another prop has occupied my time." "Fire" twice after the first verses, four times after the last one. Lots of gorgeous Neil-type electric guitar and bass & drums all around and within the verse-chorus stuff (as opposed to the Byrds-type guitars & rhythm section more typical of R.E.M.; ah, the musical language of rock, like jazz or blues it constantly reinvents itself out of the pieces of itself, delightful the way the personalities of individual contributors become incorporated into the collective environment, the ongoing ever-changing and never-changing river of sound, I mean 74.2% of all contemporary rock and roll vocals have Buddy Holly's DNA in them somewhere).

What does it all add up to?

I mean (same old question), why do I like this record? The lyrics give me the creeps, frankly, and no, I don't particularly identify with them. But I guess I identify with something that's underneath them: the singer or persona's discomfort with himself ("self-hatred" is probably not too strong a word), with the lies he tells not just in his words but in his actions and inactions, and the choking inarticulate cries of pure feeling ("Fire!") that this loud ambiguous celebration of his discomfort pulls out of him. He is raging at God (or himself) regarding his own inability to love; on some further level he is also expressing and despairing at his inability to really rage. The feeling of absence of feeling. It's twisted. Crossed wires. Emotions crackle like yellow static even though the actual sound of the record is crisp and clean and deep blue. It still feels and sounds like a love song even as the content of words and vocal try to make clear that it isn't, really. Finally what comes through is a tremendous (surprising, affecting, and appropriate whether one is following the songwriter's intentions or not) sense of longing.

"Berry-Buck-Mills-Stipe." That's the songwriter credit, and I really like it. We are a group. A gestalt. All creative contributions even out and are equal and immeasurable, because we proclaim it so (to our accountants as well as our public). Or: all songs are credited equally because we know that the actual creation takes place in *performance.* Whatever. This song, like so much R.E.M., reeks of Michael Stipe's personality conceptually, and yet one suspects that Stipe or this song without the rest of R.E.M. would be about as interesting as (forgive my prejudices) Bryan Ferry. There's no *explaining* the music that wraps itself around these words or the incredible attractiveness somehow created as a result. Why Neil Young chords? No answer. Intuition. Inspiration. It's a gestalt. Does it work? Yes it does. Listen. Listen. Listen. A sense of longing. A reaching out. An acknowledgment of the inability to reach out. A half million people being touched anyway, R.E.M.'s first hit single.

Same old answer: articulating our inarticulateness. Words clear as crystal but still their gist is mumble mumble. Oh thanks a lot. Some kind of sonic magic. Just absolutely drenched in, drowning in, the sounds and colors and textures of dissatisfied longing. It doesn't add up. Another prop. Yes, but you know I think I'm feeling something.

*First release:* IRS-53171, August 1987

# 98 The Waterboys

## *Fisherman's Blues*

Once upon a time, before the music industry became the record industry, songs were what mattered, and Top 40 charts reported sales of sheet music. In the rock era, with kids attached umbilically to portable transistor radios or Walkmen, every car with its stereo blasting, boomboxes growing from urban shoulders, *sound* has become preeminent; but a great song is still the starting point of every great record. "Fisherman's Blues," written by Mike Scott and Steve Wickham, is a magnificent song so well performed by the Waterboys (and given such a singular, enchanting, unforgettable sound) that it's hard at first to imagine anyone else recording it. And yet, as Scott and the Waterboys acknowledge on the B-side of this single (Leon Payne's "Lost Highway," immortalized by Hank Williams), great songs are made to be sung again and again by succeeding generations of singers, even though the "perfect" recording of said song may already have been accomplished. Songs live in performance. The Waterboys' recording of "Fisherman's Blues" may be impossible to improve on, but still if I played guitar I know I'd find solace and welcome relief in strumming and singing it for myself, fingers and voice stumbling clumsily but joyously (with the ecstatic union of Steve Wickham's fiddle and Tony Thistlethwaite's mandolin no doubt keening along in the memory cells of my body and brain).

I can go either way with this record: rhapsodize about the spontaneous genius of the sound (perfect down-the-middle rock and roll drumming, and the glorious sensation of "tumblin' on the sea" created by the counterpoint between regular rhythm section—drums, bass, guitar—and caterwauling harmonic/melodic section, fiddle, mandolin, and whooping voice) . . . or rave about the brilliant conscious accomplishment of the composition. Taking the latter course for a moment, I assert that Scott has crafted lyrics here worthy of Bob Dylan at his best (indeed he acknowledges Dylan—"Outlaw

Blues"—in his title and opening line). His theme is one of the most powerful threads in British/Scottish/Irish and American literature: ocean (and train! ship of the inlands) as symbol of spiritual freedom, release from the bondage of material, everyday life. His language is spare, fresh, rhythmic, and miraculously evocative: "far away from dry land/and its bitter memories" "no ceiling bearing down on me" "crashing headlong into the heartlands . . ." These lines are meant to be sung, we feel the train hurtling down through the night (and the rain), and hear (unconsciously) the rhymes between individual notes of the melody and specific word-sounds and vocalizations of word-sounds. We move rapidly across the geography of the speaker's longings, and know in our bones if not our minds that what we're hearing is prayer: "I know I will be loosened/From bonds that hold me fast/That the chains all hung around me/ Will fall away at last . . ." And we feel throughout our beings the joy and dignity and power of the singer's assertion, which is simultaneously a prayer for earthly deliverance (freedom here and now) and an allusion to the liberation and spiritual triumph that death will bring (not because we go to another place but because we know in that moment of release that we have in fact fully accomplished our work here—sez me, not Scott; each listener fills in his own received truth). The chorus says it all in eight words and perhaps a dozen notes: "Light in my head! You in my arms!" ("Whoo-oooh!")

A classic. And, sadly, but typically of the ending of the vinyl era, one that got away. Not a hit. Great opening track of the album/CD, but if I'd been fifteen in 1988 I imagine I could have been torn right open by hearing this on the airwaves, could have found some sort of anchor in the turbulence by owning it as a single and playing it over and over and over late lonely nights by my phonograph. As I do in '92 at forty-four, but I had to search hard for this seven-inch, it didn't jump out at me from every corner as equally great records often did in my 1960's adolescence. Oh, well. It changes. For worse and better. And the music remains.

Song. Song and sound. Like wind and water, they can't be separated. And they have made this dry land reality not just a richer place, but an endurable one. "Light in my head . . ."

*First release:* Chrysalis ENY 621 (U.K.), May 1988

# 99

## Neil Young

# *Rockin' in the Free World*

The death of rock and roll. Well deserved. Leave it to Neil Young to sum it all up in one bitter, uncompromising, off-the-wall, unshakable image:

I see a woman in the night
With a baby in her hand . . .
Now she puts the kid away and she's gone to get a hit
She hates her life and what she's done to it
There's one more kid that will never go to school
Never get to fall in love, never get to be cool
Keep on rockin' in the free world

I get a physical feeling in my chest and throat and around my eyes every time I hear these words (and the hard-rocking music that accompanies them). It's adrenaline, anger, bitterness, a dangerous sort of righteous emotion (with an edge of violent joy, I admit) that makes me want to smash my fist through a wall. A momentary willingness/desire to burn down everything that's corrupt in my life and my civilization. "Keep on rockin' . . ." Neil's 1989 sarcasm is clearly and appropriately aimed at those in the West who feel self-righteous about the fall of Communism. Three cheers for the free world, indeed. But it's also about the musical movement that has become one of the primary international symbols of the Western/"free enterprise" lifestyle. Rock and roll. Symbol of (as Neil says in the title of the album this single starts and finishes) freedom. And, he seems to be saying, and I heartily agree, freedom without responsibility, without caring, without awareness, is a very ugly thing. Keep on rockin' in the free world . . .

Everything gets old. And anything can be reborn. But not everything will be. There is hope, however, as long as we can look into the heart of our own ugliness and self-dishonesty and see it for what it is (and be moved to make changes). I wish this record had been a #1 hit. But I wonder how many enthusiastic rock fans would still have missed the point.

Rock and roll is not dead. But maybe it should be. Everything turns into its opposite after a while; the noise that breaks open and challenges the facade of our reality becomes in time an important part of the facade, sedating us and reinforcing our imprisonment behind the walls of illusion. I'm not saying the primary purpose of (real) rock and roll is political. I'm saying the primary purpose of all art is personal awakening, and that complacency and laziness and self-pity and fear of self-honesty create a death in life, a state of mind that rapidly turns all input to Muzak. I guess I'm saying rock and roll is a set of values. That's obviously a personal opinion, but hey, who sold you on the idea that there is such a thing as an opinion that isn't personal? Let's start from zero here.

Rock and roll is not dead. Neil Young's next album after *Freedom, Ragged Glory* (1990), is the loudest and finest of his career so far. Great music is happening even as I write and you read, around the corner in some club with bad lighting and a minimal cover charge. Check it out. But avoid the museums please, the rock and roll halls of fame and the slick magazines that enshrine them, pretty pictures mixed with sexy ads for booze and tobacco and blue jeans. The stadium tours. The press conferences. Movies about Jimi Hendrix. TV miniseries about Johnny Rotten. Let's make a distinction please. Or choke on our own vomit, like many a rock star and advanced civilization before us.

I like the sound of Neil Young's voice. I like the apocalyptic sloppy dead-eye accuracy of Crazy Horse's bombastic accompaniment. I like the tension, maybe contradiction, between sound and message. I like the raising of unanswerable questions. I like the beat. I like the explosive guitars. I like to turn up the volume. I like the way some songs tell the truth about what goes on around here sometimes.

*First release:* Reprise 22776, 1989

# 100 Nirvana

## *Smells Like Teen Spirit*

Teen Spirit, by Mennen, was and is a heavily advertised deodorant, "The only anti-perspirant made just for teens." (This book begins and ends with a brand name. Hmm.) "Smells Like Teen Spirit" is a virtual anachronism, a rock and roll hit single in the 1990's, big enough and appealing enough to break through demographic categories and make itself noticed by the world at large. It directly resulted in the sale of more than six million albums by a previously unknown punk rock/"alternative" band, and touched off one of those cyclical hysterical scrambles by record companies to get a piece of "the new sound," "the next big thing." It's a good song. A great sound. A very funny record.

"Smells Like Teen Spirit" has its feet firmly planted in what must be the most primal rock and roll tradition: cheerful stupidity ("At the Hop," "Jailhouse Rock," "Smoke on the Water," and of course "Louie Louie") . . . combined with the parallel tradition of angry stupidity, from "Blue Suede Shoes" to "Satisfaction" to "Pretty Vacant" to Suicidal Tendencies' "Institutionalized." Note that this mood of posed dumbness is perfectly communicated by the crunching riff that opens and runs through the record, and by the sound of the singer's voice. The few lyrics that come through clearly, "Here we are now/ Entertain us!" and "hello hello hello hello" and "Oh well, whatever, nevermind" perfectly support the effect. It's the loudest, meanest-sounding record ever to break out of the "alternative" ghetto—and also the most lovable (although the Violent Femmes' first album deserves a nod in this department). It's also—and every person who responds to the song knows this intuitively, even as they revel in its loud silly dumbness—fiercely, wickedly intelligent.

Critics and textbooks tend to be humorless, and so when Hamlet says "To be or not to be, that is the question," we may fail to notice that this is satire, Shakespeare making fun of

Hamlet and himself and all of us. "Smells Like Teen Spirit" arises, in my pompous opinion, from the odd but long-established historical convergence of punk rock and heavy metal at the street/garage band level, with the result that the dumbest and smartest elements of the rock audience find themselves thrown in the mosh pit together, unified by their anger and frustration even as the true alternative types recognize that the metallists subscribe heartily to the very cultural values ("kill all fags!") that they (the weirdos) are oppressed by. As a grunge rock band, well might you wonder who you're singing to, or for, or (finally) who you are. And this song addresses the issue hilariously (skewering not only the stoned obliviousness of the bands' musical and lyrical stance but also the goofy uncomprehending enthusiasm of their right on high school girl and boy fans), and with an imaginative creativity and facility with words (and vocal phrasing and instrumental phrasing) approaching genius (imagine that the speaker is complaining about the mind control of, say, a Guns n' Roses video on MTV, and the ads that precede and follow it, and the passive response of the kids watching):

> Let me at them, this is dangerous!
> "Here we are now, entertain us"
> I feel stupid, and contagious
> "Here we are now, entertain us . . ."
> A mulatto—an albino—a mosquito—my libido—

Funny, funny words, that last bit of nonsense worthy of a Shakespeare or an Edward Lear, funny and terrifyingly, and so satisfyingly, *smart.* This is what rock and roll is about. Make a loud noise. Make us feel good. Make us laugh at ourselves. Make us question ourselves. Help us feel within ourselves the power we have, individually and collectively, to redefine and recreate this absurd reality we find ourselves caught in. Remind us that we have within us a noise bigger than the outward noise that oppresses us. Redistribute authority. "Let me at them!" A call to revolution. We're too far gone to stop now.

*First release:* DGC S5 (UK), November 1991

# *CRAWDADDY! Returns*

Paul Williams founded the first U.S. rock music magazine, *Crawdaddy!,* in 1966 when he was 17. (*Rolling Stone* came along a year and a half later.) *Crawdaddy!*'s purpose was to take advantage of our common enthusiasm for and interest in new music as a basis for intimate and honest communication. Its record reviews were always personal essays exploring the experience of listening to this music. The idea was that such communication could be a basis for a sense of community. *Crawdaddy!* was always more of an underground press mag than a commercial venture.

Now Williams has revived *Crawdaddy!* (which went out of business in 1979 after a number of non-Williams incarnations) in a personal newsletter format. The first issue is 16 pages long and consists primarily of a long essay by the editor discussing R.E.M.'s brilliant album *Automatic for the People,* with commentary on other recent records by Bob Dylan, Neil Young, Bruce Cockburn, Sonya Hunter, and Television. The tone is informal and passionate. The publication is dedicated to serving the spirit of music, that which rewards us and inspires us as we listen. It is not meant to serve the music business, and will take no advertising.

## Send for a Free Sample

You can obtain a free sample of *Crawdaddy!* by sending your name and address (stamps and a self-addressed envelope are welcome but not compulsory) to:

Crawdaddy!
100 Best Singles Sample Offer
Box 611
Glen Ellen, CA 95442